Christmas 1991

lots of love from Annette
x o x

AUTOMOBILES OF THE SIXTIES

AUTOMOBILES OF THE SIXTIES

TIMOTHY JACOBS

MALLARD PRESS

First published in the United States of
America in 1991 by The Mallard Press.
Mallard Press and its accompanying design
and logo are trademarks of BDD Promotional Company, Inc.

ISBN 0-7924-5585-1

Printed in Hong Kong

Designed by Tom Debolski
Captioned by Timothy Jacobs

All pictures are courtesy of the respective
manufacturers with the following
exceptions:
© American Graphic Systems Picture
  Archives 15 (both), 26, 27, 30, 32, 40
  (left), 50, 58, 66, 69 (right), 72, 74 (left),
  77 (right), 78-79 (both), 80 (left), 84 (left),
  89 (both), 99 (right), 101 (right), 108 (left),
  113 (both), 115 (right)
Neill Bruce 120-121 (both), 124
Andrew Clarke Collection 126-127 (all)
Custom Car 56-57
CW Editorial 118 (top right), 122 (bottom
  left)
© Tom Debolski 6, 14, 23, 24, 36 (bottom),
  43(top), 48, 49, 61 (bottom), 62, 68 (left),
  73 (both), 87, 108 (right), 115 (left)
© Ruth DeJauregui 11, 13, 91
Hilton Press Services 119
© W Jeanne Kidd 38, 52, 55, 77 (left)
Andrew Morland 118 (top left)
Richard Spiegelman 110-111
TPS/Colour Library International 106-107
  (left), 117
© Nicky Wright 68-69 (center), 118 (bottom),
  123, 125 (both)
© Bill Yenne 7, 22 (both), 25, 71, 86

Page 1: **A 1961 Oldsmobile Dynamic
Eighty-Eight Holiday coupe. Note the hard-
top-style roof, sans window pillars.**

Page 2: **A 1968 Chevrolet Corvette, evi-
dencing its aerodynamic 'Mako Shark'
silhouette—a sleek surprise for car buffs
that year.**

CONTENTS

At left: A 1968 Pontiac GTO two-door hard-top. It was representative of one of the most-publicized of the 1960s 'muscle car' lines. The 1968 GTO had a top-level 400-ci (6.5-L) V-8 of 350 hp.

THE DAWNING OF THE AGE

The 1960s were the decade of *Hair*, *Mary Poppins*, *Who's Afraid of Virginia Woolf?* and *The Sound of Music*. Even so, one of the most popular entertainments of the decade was motorsports, and the average driver found the marketplace to be a cornucopia.

Automobiles in the 1960s evinced changes that were not merely extensions of the styles of the 1950s, they were also extensions of a way of thinking. Part of this lay in the strange psychologies that were produced by the Cold War. Think of the 'cloak and dagger' aspect of the apparently serene exteriors of many of the muscle cars of the mid-1960s.

Even so, the 1960s re-introduced restraint in American automotive styling, after a fashion—this caveat referring to the 'muscle cars,' whose extravagant performance belied their often-subtle exteriors. These are discussed below.

For the sake of expedience, I have classified the cars of the 1960s as several main groups: luxury cars, lower-level luxury cars, luxury muscle cars, family cars, compact cars and muscle cars.

Luxury cars offered prestige, comfort and extremely large size. Indeed, of all of them, Cadillac was the first to break the 5000-pound barrier, producing a Series 75 Fleetwood four-door sedan of 5093 pounds in 1954. The Fleetwood four-door limousine tipped the scales at 5560 pounds in 1960, was down to 5450 pounds by 1967, but had swollen anew to 5555 pounds by 1969, gaining another 100 pounds the following year.

Lincoln joined the 5000-pound club in 1959, with the four-door Capri, at 5090 pounds; the four-door Premier, at 5030 pounds; and the Continental Mark IV limousine, at 5450 pounds. I have no figures on Lincoln limousines during the 1960s, but one of the heaviest non-limousine Lincoln models was the 1967 four-door Continental convertible, a veritable rolling sun deck at 5505 pounds.

Chrysler, on the other hand, brought real weight to bear on the market with its Imperial line. The 1961 Crown Imperial four-door limousine was a hefty 5960 pounds—nearly three tons of automobile. This was paltry compared to the Crown Imperial limousines of 1963 and 1964, which crushed the scales under 6100 pounds of weight. By comparison, the 1965 Crown Imperial two-door convertible was a svelte 5345 pounds.

Lower-level luxury cars were cars that were simply the

Style would change with the decade.
Below: **A 1959 Buick Invicta sedan.**
Opposite: **The bullet-like taillights of a 1959 Cadillac.**

top-of-the-line offerings of lines that were not immediately identified with luxury. These included, for example, the Oldsmobile Ninety-Eight, the Ford LTD, the Chevrolet Caprice and so on.

By way of contrast with the true luxury cars discussed above, one of the heaviest Oldsmobiles of the 1960s was the top-of-the-line Ninety-Eight, which weighed in at 4515 pounds; and the heaviest luxury Buick of the 1960s was the 1962 Electra 225 convertible, at 4396 pounds, outweighing the Electra 225 Custom four-door hardtop of 1970, which succumbed to gravity some 4385 pounds' worth.

Since World War II, Buick had built cars that signified upward mobility by way of largeness. Several large, but tolerably designed, models carried the line through the mid-1950s, and then came the cars that gave added weight to the popular comparative, 'big as a Buick.' Already having a rather weighty appearance, Buicks really didn't need the application of massive tailfins, chrome-dripping grillework and low-slung styling: the 1958 Buick appeared to be standing still even at 100 mph—a veritable 'Spirit of Lead,' ensculpted.

Chrysler Corporation's Chrysler Division had long had a reputation for building solid, stylish automobiles. The epochal Chrysler 300s of 1955 and 1956 established a precedent for elegance and performance that was practically unmatchable. The late 1950s saw Chrysler roof-deep in the turbulent waters of the 'fins 'n chrome' wars. The leader of the Chrysler line by this time was the plush and powerful New Yorker, which would lead the line into the 1960s still bearing sweeping tailfins.

Oldsmobile was another supplier of lower-priced luxurious cars, and had long been a car for those who had attained some success, and felt satisfied with being able to own such a car.

After battling for supremacy of the race tracks with Hudson in the early 1950s, Oldsmobile paralleled Buick in its styling for the remainder of the era, up to 1959, when Buick went for waveform body surfaces, and Oldsmobile took the wide, long and very, very flat route.

There were also cars that fit into both 'muscle' and 'luxury' categories, with a dash of sportiness thrown in. After all, why shouldn't the 'upper crust' have their stake in the performance market, as well as have a hint of sprightliness thrown in? Historically, the 'luxury muscle car' was more often the norm than either the sheer muscle car or the

sheer luxury car. Thinking of some of the great makes of the past—Duesenberg, Auburn, Cord—style and performance went hand-in-hand.

In the wider view, these luxury muscle cars eventually became known as 'image cars,' intended by their owners to impart an impression of panache. At any rate, they presented an excuse for America's automakers to hearken back to the classic days of motoring, and present anew the concepts that so excited our forebears. For the 1960s, these cars were the Thunderbird, the Buick Riviera and the Oldsmobile Toronado.

Family cars formed a category that included versions of cars from all of the other categories I list here. Most commonly, they offered a touch of the roominess of luxury cars and a touch of the economy found in compact cars, though they could actually be pure representatives of any camp.

Another way to describe 1960s family cars is by their relative functionality. For instance, many medium-sized cars were used by average families simply because they were larger than compacts and cheaper than full-size cars.

However, the plainer full-size cars were not to be shunned, for you could buy a very basic large sedan for a reasonable price, too, although the most important family car of the 1960s was the station wagon.

Most station wagons had a fold-down rear seat that converted to the forward portion of the cargo deck. With the seat 'up,' you could transport a carload of kids and perhaps enough cargo to take them on a camping trip. With the seat 'down,' you could haul all the necessary materials for building that long-awaited playhouse for those very children.

Compact cars were autos like the smallest-size Ramblers, Fords and Chevrolets that promised small, easily-parkable dimensions, a low retail purchase price and comparatively low gas consumption.

In contrast to the somewhat incognito early muscle cars, compact cars were usually what they seemed to be, but some also were subject to the 'muscle car' treatment.

The Big Three—General Motors, Ford and Chrysler—and such smaller manufacturers as Studebaker and American Motors, did their best to make the public forget the awful slump in auto sales that closed out the previous decade.

Taking advantage of this slump was the encroachment

Opposite: A 1966 Oldsmobile Toronado. With hideaway headlights, front-wheel drive and a full complement of luxury features such as power steering, power brakes, and cloth, vinyl or leather interior, this was a distinctive and very plush automobile.

This luxury was combined in a sporty-looking package with a 385-hp, 425-ci (6.9 L) V-8 engine. Thus, the Toronado was an instant classic in the tradition of the luxurious and powerful Duesenbergs and Cords of the 1930s.

Hence, in this text, the Oldsmobile Toronado is classified as a 'luxury muscle car.'

upon the American market of foreign economy cars such as the Volkswagen and the Renault Dauphine. This American market niche for economy cars was actually created by America's own Rambler/American Motors lines of small cars.

On the other hand, automakers have long recognized the sales potential of performance. In the 1960s, there were the 'muscle cars'—so called because they featured powerful engines mated to gearboxes that gave every advantage to that power. These were usually cars that began their design life as a compact or medium-size coupe or sedan. The muscle cars are popularly cited as the quintessential cars of the decade, and were hybrids of the 'factory hot rods' of the 1950s, and the all-out hot rods

built by mechanics and tinkerers across the land.

For instance, oval racetracks in the early-to-mid-1950s were absolutely dominated by such 'factory hot rod' equipment as the 308-ci (five L) Hudson Hornet six-cylinder, which was, interestingly, a hemispherical combustion chamber engine of the 'flathead' type. This lead was taken over by the 331-ci (5.4 L) Chrysler hemispherical combustion chamber overhead valve V-8.

Even so, these engines were usually bolted into cars of proportionate size. Drag racers, on the other hand, had been actively stuffing huge power plants into small cars for 30 years at that point—a practice that had survived tests of its mettle in various dry lake beds, abandoned airport runways and back roads throughout the country.

factory cars in the past, but by and large, the emphasis had been mostly on top speed.

For 1958, Ford's hot power plant was the 352-ci (5.8 L) Interceptor V-8, which cranked out 265 hp with a four-barrel carburetor, and 300 hp with a four-barrel and high-compression heads. These high-output engines saw competition on the NASCAR ovals in modified form. Thus, Ford had a tradition to maintain as the 1960s loomed nearer.

Then again, there was the Chevrolet Corvette—which at first did not have enough 'muscle' to get out of its own way. The Corvette began to get some respect when Chevrolet developed a fuel injection system for their extraordinary small-block 283 (4.7 L) V-8 in 1957, and would develop on to become one of the most-known muscle cars of the 1960s.

Of course, the Chrysler 300 Series cars had devoured the competition from the introduction of the 300 in 1955, when that car, with its 300-hp, 331-ci (5.4 L) hemispherical combustion chamber V-8 was the most powerful production car in the US. The following year, a 300B, armed with the standard 300 engine for that year—a 340-hp, 345-ci (5.6 L) 'hemi' V-8—set the World Passenger Car Speed Record at Daytona, with an extended run averaging 139.9 mph.

The following year, a 375-hp, 392-ci (6.4 L) hemi V-8 made its debut in the 300C, continuing the fire-breathing tradition. This engine was mated to a snappy Torqueflite automatic. Electronic fuel injection was offered on the 300D engines of 1958, producing 390 hp from the 392 (6.4 L) hemi: dual quad carburetors on the same engine produced 380 hp.

Before the potential market for smaller bodies with these potent engines could be tapped, however, the AMA (Automobile Manufacturers' Association) decided to de-emphasize racing for American cars in 1957, and set up strict guidelines that allowed large engines, but also reinforced the notion of large carbodies to go with them.

Some companies were not to be denied a fiscal shot in the arm if they could get it. One of the most highly-publicized muscle cars was born in circumstances that have become part of the apocrypha of the 1960s, when, in 1963, under cover even from their own directors, John De Lorean and several other Pontiac personnel developed the legendary Pontiac GTO. The full story is given in a subsequent chapter.

Opposite: **A slightly-modified 1961 Corvette. The standard engine for this car was a 230-hp, 283-ci (4.7 L) V-8. Later Corvettes would house more potent power plants—and, according to the dictates of the marketplace, they would have to—as a performance car, the Corvette had numerous competitors both in the market and at the race track.**

Some of the Corvette's more feared competitors were the Shelby Mustangs. These were Ford products that had been specially equipped and tuned by race-car builder Carroll Shelby.

One of the later Shelby Mustangs was the GT 500 convertible, which boasted a 355-hp, 428-ci (seven L) V-8. *Above:* **A 1968 Shelby GT 500 Mustang. This was a classic late-1960s 'muscle car.'**

Then, the establishment of the National Hot Rod Association (NHRA) and the American Hot Rod Association (AHRA) created legitimate venues for drag racing.

Also, the legitimization of stockcar racing by such official sanctioning bodies as the National Association for Stock Car Auto Racing (NASCAR) made a place for the highly modified, but deceptively mild-looking, road machines that had been developed by bootleggers and moonshiners to elude the law over the winding back-country roads of the rural US.

In fact, drag racing was to be an important promotion tool for automakers, and the increasing importance of low elapsed times at the dragstrip fostered the development of the big-engine/little carbody schema of the muscle car. Gone, then, was the dominion of large cars with large engines that could take their time getting to top speed.

Therefore, the drag racing concept of low elapsed time unveiled a new horizon of potential sales weapons for US automakers. Granted, there had been some fairly quick

TIGHTWADS, CRUSHING ISSUES AND A HINT OF MUSCLE

One of the catchphrases of the turn of the decade into the 1960s was 'compact car.' With the turn of the decade, a recession was upon the US, and a sizable market opened up for economy cars. In 1959, Rambler, then America's fourth-ranked automaker, posted record profits of $60,341,823, much of it based on the company's compact, economical, American line. In fact, the resale value of Ramblers was among the very highest in the US, connoting the esteem in which these cars were held by the public. Dependable, economical and cute as the little cars were, they opened up the market for small cars in the US, just after an era in which it seemed that nothing but big cars would sell.

America's 'Big Three' automakers saw this as an opportunity as well as a challenge. Soon, Rambler had competition in the domestic compact market from such new makes as the Ford Falcon, the Plymouth Valiant, the Chevrolet Corvair, the Chevy II, the Dodge Lancer (later supplanted by the reconceived Dart), the Mercury Comet, the Buick Special, the Pontiac Tempest and the Studebaker Lark.

The catchy little sales ditty 'When You're Driving in a Rambler,' set to the tune of 'When You're Smiling,' drove home the point that Ramblers were trouble-free, and would serve Rambler well in its compact car battles with the Big Three—whose own products not infrequently evidenced instabilities of various kinds.

The first Rambler American, introduced in 1958, was practically a reprise of the 1955 Nash Rambler. Essentially a rounded box, it had rear wheel well cutouts that looked as if they had been cut too far to the back, and not far enough forward, making the carbody look slightly out of sync with the chassis. It was powered by a 195.6-ci (3.2 L) six-cylinder engine of 90 hp.

The Rambler American remained basically the same for the next year, 1959, and was available in sedan and station wagon models. Rambler achieved net sales of $869,849,704—in large part because of the growing recession, a boon for the small car market.

The year 1960 saw the introduction of the Custom line, which supplanted the Super as the classiest American. Four-door sedans were offered in all three ranges, in addition to the two-door sedan and station wagon models, with the extra offering of a two-door business coupe in the low-price Deluxe range. The engine was the same as that of

Opposite: **A 1961 Rambler American convertible. At the turn of the decade, the Rambler American was the leading economy car line in the US. Powered by a 90-hp, 195.6-ci (3.2 L) six cylinder engine, Americans got good gas mileage—and, at 173.1 inches in length, they fit into almost** *any* **parking space.**

previous years, but the options now also included an overdrive transmission; foam rubber seat cushions; a heavy-duty suspension system; a 'Twin grip' differential; a padded dash; windshield washers; and more.

The lowest factory price for a 1960 Rambler American was $1781, and the highest price was $2235—representing the difference between a Deluxe two-door business coupe and a Custom station wagon.

In 1961, the American got a major styling revision, with somewhat severely squared-off front and rear profiles and a bolder molding crease along the sides. As compared to the previous overall length of 178.25 inches, the new American measured out at 173.1 inches. It was therefore easier to park, and well-established as the way to go for economy.

It was the last year for the Super model, which would be replaced the next year with the 400. Four-door station wagon models in every level, as well as convertible models

in the Custom series, made their appearance. The essential differences between the Deluxe, Super and Custom lines were as follows.

The Deluxe offered, as standard equipment, front arm rests; a front ash tray; a cigar lighter; dual sun visors; black floor mats; and black cargo mats for station wagons. The Super came standard with all of same; plus rear door armrests; a rear ashtray; colored floor mats; colored rubber cargo mats for station wagons; automatic courtesy lights; a luggage rack for station wagons; foam-cushion front seats; and a chrome horn ring.

The Custom models had all of same, plus an oil bath air cleaner; colored passenger compartment carpets for station wagons; dual horns; a two-tone steering wheel; and extra-fancy hubcaps.

Of course, America's other automakers were not taking this passively. Studebaker, already on its way down and further victimized by a sagging national economy, came out with their Lark series in 1959. These were friendly-looking, squared-off little cars of 175 inches overall length in sedan and four-door models, and 184.5 inches in station wagon models. Two levels of trim were offered—Deluxe and Regal.

Equipped with a 169-ci (2.7 L) six-cylinder engine of 90 hp the first year, and with an upgraded version of same—rated at 112 hp—in 1961, Larks were optionally offered with a 259-ci (4.2 L) V-8 of 180 hp the first year. Two V-8 options—the 259, and a 289-ci (4.7 L) engine of 225 hp—were offered the second year.

Lark models included two- and four-door sedans, plus two-door wagons and a special model called the Economiler four-door sedan, which had a unique 179-inch overall length. A convertible was offered with Regal trim in 1961. The addition of quad headlights for most Larks in 1961 was augmented by such features as sun roofs in some cars.

The Rambler American and the Studebaker Lark had stiff competition from General Motors, Ford and Chrysler. In the mid-1950s, Ed Cole of Chevrolet's design department dreamed of creating a car that would incorporate aircraft-like features, for a better-than-average ratio of structural strength to weight, and enhanced compactness.

In particular, he dreamed of a Chevrolet that would incorporate unit-body construction—an aircraft concept that was borne out in several other American cars and a

great many European autos. With such construction, one could be freer with one's design ideas, as the body and chassis, being essentially melded, were stronger and lighter than the common, separate body-and-chassis designs.

Also, such a car, if sufficiently small, would benefit from having an air-cooled engine—another aircraft idea that had been successfully used by such imported cars as the Volkswagen. Independent front and rear suspension—a distinctly European touch—would give such a car smooth riding qualities, and would cut down on production costs.

The Corvair was Chevrolet's first compact competitor for the Rambler. General Motors pulled out all the stops, presenting a car with a sophisticated sort of European flair with a soapcake-like, boxy body that was thereafter emulated throughout the world by such automakers as BMW. The Corvair was first presented to the public in late 1959.

In keeping with the fashion of most American cars in the 1950s–60s, Corvairs had four headlamps. All models, including the station wagon that was introduced in 1961, were built on the same 108-inch wheelbase chassis. The first year Corvair offered a choice of four-door sedan or two-door club coupe. The top-of-the-line Corvair had a factory price tag of $2103 in 1960.

The year 1961 saw the introduction of increased ranges for the Corvair, each range connoting a level of comparative luxury. Beginning with the leanest accommodation, there was the Series 500, which offered a four-door sedan, a club coupe and a station wagon. Series 700 cars offered the same configurations, with more luxurious interiors and trim, and more options.

Above these were the Monza sedan and club coupe, sporting the widest range of convenience options and performance options for the engine; the Greenbriar Sport Wagon, an upscale station wagon; and the Corvan, a small van available with or without side windows and removable extra seats.

Ford brought out the Falcon line in 1960, as a direct competitor to Chevrolet, Rambler, Dodge and Plymouth. With an overall length of 181.2 inches for sedans and 189 inches for station wagons, Falcon was nearly three feet shorter than a full-size Ford. The first-year Falcon had extremely simple styling, with dual headlights, a minimum of trim lines and a minimum of options.

These cars were underpowered with an 85-hp, 144-ci

Above: A promotional photo of a 1959 Studebaker hardtop coupe. The Lark was Studebaker's new compact line for that year. The power plant that first year was a 169-ci (2.7 L) in-line six cylinder of 90 hp, with an optional 259-ci (4.2 L) V-8 available.

At left: A 1960 Lark VI convertible and a 1960 Lark VIII station wagon. As is indicated, the former had a six-cylinder power plant and the latter had a V-8. The engine range for 1960 Larks was increased to include an optional 289-ci (4.7 L) V-8 of 225 hp.

(2.3 L) six-cylinder engine. Transmission options were a standard-shift three speed and an automatic two-speed. Electric windshield wipers and two-tone paint were among the limited options offered. The public loved the conservatively-styled Falcon, and distrusted the Corvair: the first-year market records of both cars saw the Falcon trouncing the Corvair in sales.

The cheapest Corvair you could buy in 1960 had a factory price of $1984. Ford, having long practiced the underpricing gambit, factory-priced their lowest-level Falcon at precisely $10 cheaper, or $1974.

Ford added the upscale Futura to the Falcon sedan and station wagon offerings for 1961. The Futura was a two-door coupe with bucket seats and a center console. An optional 170-ci (2.8 L) six with 101 hp gave second-year Falcons a bit more pep.

Ford Motor Company introduced the Mercury Comet in 1960. The Comet was downright flashy in its styling—as compared to the Falcon—with slanting 'cat's eye' taillights, sprightly tailfins and quad headlights. It was armed with the same 144-ci (2.3 L), 85-hp six as the Falcon.

In fact, the Comet was first six-cylinder car ever offered

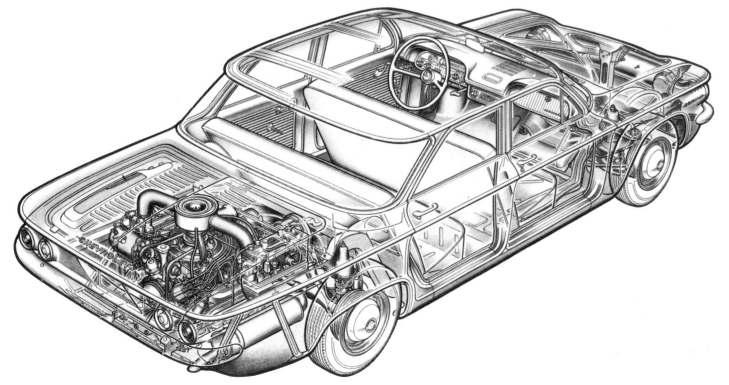

Chevrolet's early-1960s entry into the economy car market was the Corvair. *At left:* A cutaway view of a 1960 Corvair. Introduced in 1960, the Corvair was unusual for an American car in that it had a rear-mounted engine and all-independent suspension.

The first-year power plant was a 140-ci (2.2-L) horizontally-opposed six-cylinder engine of 80 hp.

Above: A 1960 Corvair 500 sedan. This was the base trim level Corvair.

Opposite: A 1960 Corvair 700 sedan. Its exterior chrome trim identifies it as a 'deluxe' trim level car. The Monza was the top of the line for that year, with bucket seats and a sun roof.

by Mercury. Essentially, the Comet looked like a dressed-up Falcon, and its running gear was much the same. Mercury advertised the Comet as a 'family-sized' compact. Oddly enough, the Comet sedans were longer than the station wagons, at 194 inches, compared to 191 inches, in overall length.

A slightly more potent six was optional for 1961—a 170-ci (2.7 L) power plant producing 101 hp. The Comet S-22 series was introduced as a fancy trim package.

The base factory price for a 1961 Rambler American two-door, six person Custom station wagon was $2080. By comparison, a comparable Studebaker Lark two-door wagon was $2290, a Ford Falcon two-door wagon was $2225 and a Corvair two-door wagon was $2266.

While Rambler, Studebaker, Ford Motor Company and General Motors were thus garnering their share of the compact-car market, Chrysler Corporation was not to be denied, and launched a two-pronged attack with almost identical cars, offered through its Dodge and Plymouth divisions.

The first of these, offered to the market in 1960, was the Valiant. This line was first considered to be autonomous, but was made one of the Plymouth line in 1961. It had an oddball fastback look with a spare tire cover stamped into the trunk lid. Valiants came in two trim levels, V-100 and V-200, and types included two four-door sedans (one of which was actually a pillarless hardtop design) and one four-door station wagon for both the V-100 and V-200 ranges.

The 1960 Valiant power plant was a 101-hp, 170.9-ci (2.8 L) six-cylinder. A three-speed manual transmission was standard, and power train options included a three-speed automatic and an engine option called 'Hyper Pack,' which increased the power plant's compression and added a four-barrel carburetor—boosting output to 148 hp.

Valiants of 1961 were much the same as the originals, but they were now known officially as 'Plymouth Valiants,' and a two-door sedan variant replaced one of the four-door hardtop variants. Replaced, but not dropped entirely, this same four-door hardtop was offered as a line of its own—the Valiant Signet.

An optional engine was made available—this was the 148-hp, 225-ci (3.6 L) slant six engine that would become a Chrysler Corporation legend for its reliability.

In 1961, Dodge brought out the Lancer, a compact car that was virtually identical to the Valiant, but had classier trim and interior treatments. The two trim levels for the Lancer were the 170 Series and the 770 Series. Engine choices were the same as for the Valiant. The Lancer survived only one more year; then Dodge made the formerly mid-sized Dart its compact car.

In 1961, General Motors, not satisfied with the marketplace performance of the Corvair, turned out two compacts through their Buick and Oldsmobile divisions, both of which were powered by 155-hp, 215-ci (3.5 L) aluminum-block V-8s. These unique little engines had an appeal of their own. The cars in question—the Buick Special and the Oldsmobile F-85—bore the styling imprint of their parent companies, and shared a 112-inch wheelbase.

Both offered coupes, sedans and station wagons. The two levels of Special trim were represented by Special Standard and Special Deluxe, which included the top-of-the-line Skylark Sport Coupe; and the same values were identified in the F-85 with F-85 Standard and F-85 Deluxe, which included the *nonpareil* Cutlass Sport Coupe.

Ford Motor Company's early-1960s offering for the compact car market was the simple but somewhat stylish Ford Falcon, with its companion line, the Mercury Comet.

Opposite: **A 1960 Ford Falcon four-door station wagon. With a 144-ci (2.3-L) six-cylinder engine, the Falcon offered good economy, but was a bit underpowered. The station wagon models allowed ample of room for cargo.**

Above: **A 1960 Falcon Deluxe two-door sedan. Over the years, the Falcon would go through various permutations, but would be billed as a compact car.**

The Plymouth Valiant was introduced in 1960. In the ensuing decade, Valiants acquired a reputation for reliability matched by few other cars.

Below: A 1960 Valiant V-200 sedan. This car was powered by a 170-ci (2.7 L) version of the legendary slant six, and floor shift was standard.

The Pontiac Tempest was almost as unusual as the Corvair, with a rear-mounted transaxle and a flexible driveshaft. Its front-mounted four-cylinder engine was essentially a 389-ci (6.4-L) V-8 cut in half. The upper-level Tempest was the LeMans, with bucket seats. *Opposite:* A 1961 Tempest LeMans.

Transmission options for both included the standard offering of three-speed manual, and optional automatic or four-speed manual (for Skylark only). The F-85 had an advantage over the Skylark's four-speed 'stick' by dint of a performance option that boosted the F-85 V-8's horsepower to 185.

Having produced one rear-engine compact and two with aluminum engines, General Motors was clearly intrigued with the idea of producing unique compact cars—as the Pontiac Tempest of 1961 further attested.

Powered by a 194.5-ci (3.1 L) four-cylinder, the Pontiac Tempest was offered in its first year with a flexible 'rope' driveshaft, torque-tube drive, a rear-mounted transaxle and independent rear suspension. Transmission offerings were three-speed manual, four-speed synchro-mesh

(manual) or two-speed automatic, with the 110-hp engine set up for 10 more horsepower if the automatic was used.

The Tempest had a typical Pontiac split grille, deep sidebody creases and an overall length of 189 inches. Standard and Custom trim levels both featured four-door sedan, two-door coupe and four-door ('Safari') station wagon models, with the Custom two-door coupe being designated as the Le Mans.

Performance option packages offered a four-barrel version of the four, producing 155 hp, or a Buick aluminum V-8 of the same horsepower rating.

At the opposite end of the spectrum from these compacts were cars that gave the 1960s yet another dimension. These were the large, well-cushioned luxury cars with gigantic engines that continued the 'behemoth' image

The name Cadillac has long been synonymous with luxury, both in America and throughout the world.

This page: two views of a sleek 1960 Cadillac Series 6200 convertible. This example shows that, while the 6200 was the low Cadillac trim level, it need never have stood second to any in terms of *elegance*.

The 6200 had power windows and power seats, and its optional equipment included air conditioning, electric door locks and tinted glass.

that had been established for upper-level American cars in the late 1950s. The cream of the American luxury crop in the 1960s were General Motors' Cadillac, Ford's Lincoln Continental and Chrysler's Imperial—truly massive automobiles, as I have previously discussed.

The Cadillac's history goes back to the inception of the Cadillac Company in 1902. Including such ground-breaking innovations as the electric starting motor, interchangeability of parts, and the first standard-equipment closed carbodies, Cadillac built up a heady reputation for itself over the years. With such elegant and luxurious makes as Packard and Pierce-Arrow as competitors, Cadillac early on learned the modes and methods of luxury carbuilding.

Regularly offering standard equipment that was equal to most other manufacturers' highest option packages, Cadillac literally began its designs where others left off. Also,

Cadillac pioneered the tailfin, that aspect of automobilia that so dominated the late 1950s.

In the early 1960s, Cadillacs still had tailfins—long, low and sharp at the nether end. The cars themselves had a long, low look. That's not all, for *Car Life* magazine of 1960 selected the Cadillacs of that year as the best buy in the luxury car field. The bottom of the Cadillac line was the Series 6200, which offered three four-door sedans, a two-door coupe, and a convertible. The standard passenger capacity was six persons, and standard luxury items included power steering; power brakes; an automatic transmission; dual backup lamps; windshield washers; and dual speed wipers.

The convertible offered optional power windows and two-way power seats, and general optional equipment included air conditioning and a host of other convenience items that would add even more luxury and embellishment to the Cadillacs of this year.

The more upscale DeVille offerings included power windows and power seats among their standard items. For the record, Cadillac factory prices started at $5080 for a four-door, six-window 6200 and moved up to $5498 for the same car of the DeVille series.

A little higher in the price range, at $7401 for a six-person hardtop coupe, was the legendary Eldorado, the Cadillac line that made heads turn. The Eldorado for 1960 offered no dramatic styling departure from its DeVille and 6200 brethren, other than additional refinements in trim and a generally more subtle and elegant appearance.

Standard items on the Eldorado were, in addition to those cited for the models above, fog lamps; a remote-control trunk lock; a radio with antenna and rear speaker; power vent windows; a six-way power seat; air suspension system; electric door locks; Cruise Control; a Guide-Matic headlight dimmer; air conditioning; E-Z Eye glass; and the Eldorado engine—a 390-ci (6.4 L) power plant with 345 hp (a gain of 20 hp over the lower-priced models).

Interior trim was a choice of cloth or leather or a combination of the two. It should be said that, even though a higher level of Cadillac offerings existed, the Eldorado four-door, six-passenger Brougham topped the Cadillac price list at $13,075—approximately what one would pay in the 1990s for a mid-level Chevrolet. Eldorado offerings for 1960 included a hardtop coupe, the Biarritz convertible and the six-passenger Brougham.

The 'King of the Mountain' here was the Fleetwood series—the cars that diplomats, presidents, royalty and Very Important Persons of all kinds rode in. Fleetwood offerings for 1960 included the low-price ($6233) Series 60 Special Fleetwood, a four-door, six-passenger sedan; and the Series 6700 Fleetwood Seventy-Five, including a four-door, nine-passenger sedan and a four-door, nine-passenger limousine, the latter of which was priced at $9748.

The nine-passenger Fleetwoods had high-headroom six-window styling; auxiliary jump seats; a broad-ribbed roof edge; and a full range of options. The chauffeur's compartment was finished in Florentine leather, while the passenger compartment was finished in either Bradford cloth or Bedford cloth, both in combinations with wool. A full range of options topped out the list for these very prestigious Cadillacs. (The Eldorado V-8 was an option for these, as well as for any, Cadillac model.)

Above: A 1962 Cadillac Series 6200 four-door, four-window sedan. Note the pillarless 'hardtop' design: all Series 6200 sedans for that year were hardtops.

The top of the Cadillac line was the Fleetwood series. At 242 inches, the Fleetwoods were 20 inches longer than the Series 6200 cars and, at 5325 pounds for a four-door sedan, outweighed comparable Series 6200 cars by almost 700 pounds.

Below: Another view of a 1962 Cadillac Series 6200 four-door, four-window sedan. See also the rear view of this car on page 23.

Ford Motor Company's luxury car was the Lincoln, the top level of which was the Continental series. *Opposite:* A 1960 Continental Mark V convertible. Tinted glass, power brakes, power steering, power windows and power seats were included as standard equipment on these cars.

The look of the Continental changed radically in 1961 (see also the Continental on page 101).

Lincoln had been Ford's answer to General Motors' Cadillac since the 1930s. Ford actually had the upper hand with the V-12 Lincoln Continentals of the 1940s, which were sleek and distinguished automobiles. Lincoln styling fell a notch or two toward mediocrity in the early 1950s, succumbing to the then-popular 'bathtub' look, which was to that era what the angular, boxy look was to the 1980s.

Then Lincoln had 'it' again, in spades, in 1956, with the elegant, simple, well-proportioned lines of the Lincoln Continental, which like its predecessor Continental, was an instant classic, recognized as a work of art around the world. The design held for another year, even as the standard Lincoln cars went the way of massive sheet metal and meat-cleaver-like fins.

The Continental of 1958, unfortunately, was also sucked into the 'bigger is better' fray, and became a metal monster just as other luxury cars of the period had become. Thus, Lincoln arrived at the brink of the 1960s. The 1960 Lincoln line featured slanted quad headlights and slashing body lines on a luxury car scale.

They were large for their era, at 227 inches overall length, and in some locales, Lincoln owners were actually required to put safety warning lights at the extremities of their cars. (Be that as it may, they were smaller than the early 1970s Cadillacs, of which several models exceeded the 250-inch mark, thus adding new meaning to the term 'full-size car.')

Each of these last of the 'fins 'n chrome' Lincolns had, as standard equipment, power brakes; power steering; a heater and defroster unit; undercoating; a clock; a radio; windshield washers; a padded dashboard; a center rear armrest; and dual exhaust pipes.

The standard Lincoln engine was, as it had been since 1958, a 430-ci (seven L) V-8 (though it had been detuned from an initial 375 hp to the 1960 standard of 315). A Turbo-Drive automatic transmission was standard, with a directed-drive differential as an optional improvement. The basic Lincoln line for 1960 offered two four-door, six-passenger sedans and one two-door, six-passenger coupe.

The next step up was the Lincoln Premier series, which offered the same body configurations, but also featured power windows and four-way power seats.

The top-of-the-line Continental Mark V featured a distinctive grille pattern (described as a 'criss-cross, dot-in-a-square' pattern); circular rear lights; front fender chrome bars and a reverse-slant, retractable rear window. Six-way power seats; tinted glass and power vent windows were also among the Mark V's standard features.

The 1960 Mark V was presented in a number of six-passenger configurations, the four-door variants being the Executive, the Town Car and two regular sedan models. The two-door variants included a coupe and a convertible. Optional equipment for all 1960 Lincolns included an air conditioner/heater unit; an electronic headlight dimmer; electric door locks; a power lubricator; an FM radio; power seat variations; a remote-control trunk lid opener; and power vent windows. The most expensive Mark V, the Executive sedan, cost $10,230, while the cheapest, the basic Lincoln two-door coupe, cost $5253.

The following year saw dramatic changes in Lincoln styling, and presented a surprise for the automotive establishment. This was the subtle, squared-off Lincoln Continental of 1961, a styling coup that set the tone for 1960s luxury cars—echoes of its lines can be found in every 1960s luxury car after that year. The Industrial Design Institute conferred its extremely prestigious Bronze Medal to the designers of the 1961 Lincoln Continental—an honor very few automobiles have ever received.

The Continental was the only Lincoln model offered in 1961, and in fact, for the remainder of the 1960s. In its first year, the new design was offered in just two variants: a four-door sedan and a four-door convertible. The doors on each opened to the center of the car, for an extra touch of elegance.

Standard equipment for the 1961 Continental was a 300-hp, 430-ci (seven L) engine; an automatic transmission; a radio with rear speaker; a heater; power brakes; power steering; power windows; walnut appliqué or padded dashboard; carpeting; and power door locks. Options included air conditioning; six-way power seats; speed control; special interior trim; and tinted windows.

The third of the 'Big Three' luxury cars was the Chrysler Imperial. Actually, while Imperial had its inception as a super-luxurious Chrysler, it became a separate division of Chrysler Corporation in 1954, and began developing its own personality in 1955 and 1956, with basic Chrysler 300 styling—given a unique twist by the device of free-standing taillights mounted atop the rear fenders.

By 1958, the Imperial had developed a long, sleek look with extra-long, powerfully sweeping tailfins that began their ascent at the rear of the front doors. Like most Chrysler products of the era, Imperials took the jet-age imagery that then abounded and went to the stratosphere with it.

By 1960, the Imperial's fins had acquired a more bulgy appearance, due to their rising abruptly from the rear quarter panel of the car on a line with the leading edge of the rear wheel wells. There were several models offered, all with 350-hp 413-ci (6.8 L) engines, and Chrysler's snappy Torqueflite automatic transmission with push-button gear selection.

However, the real news for early 1960s Imperial models appeared in 1961, with the advent of the now-famous free-standing quad headlights, framed by the front fender overhang above, the tapering grille on one side and the protruding bumper below. These headlights gave the 1961 Imperial an instantly classic look, though the abrupt tailfin persisted (only to be eliminated the following model year). No longer set atop the tailfin, the taillights were set halfway down the backs of the fins.

For 1961, Imperial offerings ranged from the lowest-level Custom to the top-of-the-line Crown Imperial (as distinguished from the middle-level Crown model). As with the 1960 cars, an unusual simulated rear canopy contrasted with the forward four-fifths of the roof surface. The Custom line offered two- and four-door hardtops, both of which were six-person cars.

The wheel well openings and rocker panels were trimmed with chrome, and power steering and power brakes were standard equipment. As with all 1961 Imperials, the power plant was a 350-hp, 413-ci (6.8 L) V-8, mated to a push-button automatic transmission.

The Crown series offered two- and four-door hardtop models, plus a two-door convertible. The Crown's standard equipment was the same as with the Custom, but also included a power seat; a rear license plate frame; a vanity mirror; carpeting; power windows; and a sideview mirror. It is worth noting that Le Barons of previous years included two-tone paint schemes as standard.

The LeBaron series had a distinctive square (as opposed to wrap-around) rear window that added a formal touch to the car's styling. LeBaron standard features included those discussed above, plus power vent windows; stone shield moldings; and whitewall tires. The 1961 LeBaron was strictly a six-person, four-door hardtop.

The 1961 Crown Imperial was an eight-passenger, four-door limousine. True to a conservative styling dictum for ultra-posh cars that had been established by such automakers as Packard in the 1920s (but was flouted by such as Duesenberg), the 1961 Imperial featured 1960 styling, and was thus denied the distinctive free-standing headlights cited above.

Air conditioning, auto pilot, automatic headlight dimmer, three heaters and power windows were included among a plethora of luxury features that were standard for this custom-built car.

The 1961 Imperials had a long list of options, including a rear-window defogger; a crankcase ventilation system;

electric door locks; stone shields and sill molding; a Flitesweep deck lid; electric Touch-Tuner radio with power antenna; Solex glass; a stainless steel fore-roof in Custom models; leather trim in Crown and LeBaron models; six-way power seats; and combinations of the above, sold as packages: Basic Group, Convenience Group and Decor Group.

The basic two-door hardtop Custom sold for $4925; the Crown four-door hardtop sold for $5649; the LeBaron sold for $6428; and the Crown Imperial sold for $16,000—about what the average American house cost eight years earlier, and approximately what a slightly toney 'economy car' costs in the 1990s.

More affordable, but still offering some luxury, were the cars offered by the Big Three in the top of their Buick, Chevrolet, Chrysler, Ford, Mercury, Oldsmobile and Pontiac lines. These were calculated to evoke the glories of the true luxury cars, but were available to those who could only dream of cruising to the bank in their Cadillac, Lincoln or Imperial.

What made this possible is that many of these cars

Another slogan Chrysler Corporation used in its Imperial promotions was '... magnificently unmatched in sheer driving virility.' This undoubtedly referred to the Imperial-standard 350-hp, 413-ci (6.8 L) V-8 engine, with a snappy Torqueflite automatic transmission to translate all that power to the rear wheels.

At left: A 1960 Imperial LeBaron four-door hardtop sedan. Power windows and two-tone paint were among the LeBaron's standard features. Also, a rectangular (rather than wraparound) rear window distinguished the LeBaron from other Imperials. At the time, it was the mid-range Imperial.

Chrysler Corporation very confusingly designated the lowest-level Imperial the Crown series, and the highest-level Imperial the Crown Imperial.

America's automakers also provided lower-level cars that offered luxury for a broader market than that of the Cadillac, Continental and Imperial.

Buick was one of the lines that notably offered comfort and size for that market. *Below:* A 1960 Buick LeSabre four-door sedan. Offered in numerous configurations, including station wagon, sedan and convertible models, the LeSabre offered a little something for everybody.

were essentially nothing more than luxuriant trim, accessory and powertrain offerings on otherwise standard chassis and bodies. Such, for instance, was the Chevrolet Caprice, the Ford LTD and the Dodge Monaco. Therefore, even the only-slightly-wealthier-than-average carbuyer could purchase his or her dream machine in the 1960s, and the family car owner could be smug in knowing that the family sedan was an upscale car at heart.

These cars kept their owners happy, at least, and the upper-level versions of them were often purchased by 'the upper crust' as second cars. These were definitely cars that could be driven to the country club, or parked outside the better stores in municipalities of those pre-shopping mall days, while their lower-priced brethren served handily—in station wagon and sedan configurations—for ferrying the average family around.

Therefore, if millionaires were not ashamed of these cars, then neither were the slightly-overreaching branch managers of department stores. Similarly, the stock clerk might find, in his base-level version of the Ford Galaxie or

the Oldsmobile Eighty-Eight (a lower-level brother to the Ninety-Eight), the seed of a dream of grandeur, as he ferried the family to 'the movies.'

The primary luxury offering from Buick from 1960 through the end of the decade was the Electra 225, though it can be argued that most Buicks were plush.

The Electra for 1960 offered two ranges—Series 4700 and Series 4800. The Series 4800 cars were given the '225' designation and were considered to be Buick's true luxury line, and three types were presented to the public: a sedan (designated 'Riviera') and a hardtop, both with four doors; and a two-door convertible. Electras were identified by their larger size, and by the four ventiports on the sides of the front fenders—as opposed to three on such lesser models as the LeSabre and Invicta, the low- and mid-range Buicks of the early 1960s.

The power plant for the Buick Electra (and the Invicta) was a standard 325-hp, 401-ci (6.6 L) V-8, with a Twin-Turbine automatic transmission. The low-level LeSabre had a 364-ci (5.9 L) engine.

Standard features of the Electra 225 (some of which were standard, some of which were options, and some of which were not available for lower-level lines) were power steering; power brakes; an adjustable speedometer; electric windshield wipers; a trip mileage indicator; a cigar lighter; dual sunshades; a foot-operated parking brake; dual horns; a single-key locking system; foam seat cushions; an electric clock; a trunk light; a deluxe steering wheel; deluxe wheel covers; license plate frames; a glove box light; backup lights; a glare-proof rearview mirror; a parking brake signal light; a safety buzzer; a map light; a two-way power seat; and power windows (for the convertible).

Optional equipment for the Electra 225, and indeed the lower-level Buicks, included air conditioning; an automatic headlight dimmer; a tissue dispenser; a compass; a visor vanity mirror; trunk and floor mats; a litter basket; six-way power seats; bucket seats; power windows; power vent windows; various types of radios with and without power antennas; a rear-seat speaker; a heater and defroster unit; tinted glass; white sidewall tires; custom moldings; two-tone finish; dual exhausts; and dual-speed windshield wipers with washers.

The Electra 225 Riviera Sedan for 1960 was factory priced at $4300. For 1961, all Buicks were restyled, with a much more streamlined, finless appearance, that included a spearhead motif that was embossed into the sheet metal at the beltline, and formed two major sheet metal creases that ran the length of both sides of the car. That same year found the familiar 'ranking signature' of three ventiports for lower-level cars and four for the Electras in existence.

The following years found the styling of the Electra branching off into a Lincoln Continental-inspired blockiness, with not quite so good a result at imitation as was attained by the Chrysler Imperial. Then again, the lower-level Buicks had actually achieved a rather light-looking appearance.

The 1960 Chrysler New Yorker had outward-flaring, batlike fins that gave it the appearance of a bird—wings outstretched—coming in for a landing. The New Yorker shared a 126-inch wheelbase with the performance-oriented 300 Series and the smaller-engined, lower-priced Saratoga.

The New Yorker had a 350-hp, 413-ci (6.8 L) V-8, mated to a Torqueflite automatic transmission. Standard equipment included power steering; power brakes; foam-cushion seats; an electric clock; a deluxe steering wheel;

Above: A 1960 Buick LeSabre two-door hardtop. The 'ventiports' that are seen on the upper front fender of this car were by then a Buick hallmark, as well as a mark of distinction among Buick owners: three ventiports indicated a lower-level Buick like the LeSabre, while four ventiports indicated an upper-level Buick like the Electra.

Compare the 1959 Buick shown on page six with the image shown here, and note how the sweeping fins of the Buick had been de-emphasized as the 1950s turned into the 1960s.

Chrysler Corporation's premier lower-level luxury line was Chrysler proper. *Below:* A promotional photo of a 1961 Chrysler Newport, a low-level Chrysler with a 265-hp, 361-ci (5.9 L) V-8.

Power steering, power brakes and power windows were among the options available for this car.

The top-level Chryslers such as the New Yorker emulated the luxury of the Imperial in the extent of their appointments.

windshield washers; a padded dashboard; a remote-control sideview mirror; backup lights; parking brake lights; map lights; stone shields; and sill moldings. Some of this equipment was standard, some of it was optional, and some of it was unavailable—for the lower-priced Chrysler lines.

New Yorkers were offered in four four-door types, including two sedans and two station wagons, and two two-door types—a coupe and a convertible. Optional equipment—which was optional also (for the most part) on the lower-level lines—included power windows; power seats; swivel seats; air conditioning; a radio with touch tuner; a rear speaker; a power antenna; an auto-pilot; an automatic headlight dimmer; a Flitesweep deck lid; a rear window defogger; a Sure-Grip differential; tinted glass; two-tone paint; a Captive Air system; and vacuum door locks.

The Chrysler 300 Series was considered a part of the New Yorker line, and supplied the most prestigious Chryslers with an added reputation for performance—in the grand style of the classic Duesenbergs, Packards and other legendary cars of the 1920s and 1930s. I discuss the

300's performance propensities elsewhere in this text. The 1960 four-door hardtop sedan had a factory price of $4518, while the 1960 two-door hardtop coupe cost $5411.

The 1959–60 Oldsmobiles had hood and trunk lids that seemed as flat and expansive as football fields. The sides of the bodies, while by no means shallow, appeared to be so in comparison with the length and breadth of the cars—which dimensions were accentuated by the flatness of the upper body surfaces.

Actually, the top-of-the-line Oldsmobiles were average in size for luxury cars of the period, with front and rear tread of 61 inches, a wheelbase of 126.3 inches and an overall length of 223 inches. The success of the Oldsmobile stylists can be measured by that fact: their cars looked longer, wider and lower than they actually were. Also, the above measurements were taken from the Ninety-Eight, which was at that point possessed of a wheelbase that was 4.6 inches longer than the lower-level Super Eighty-Eight and Dynamic Eighty-Eight models.

For 1960, the Oldsmobile Ninety-Eight lost 2.1 inches in overall length, but its wheelbase and width remained the same. If anything, the lines of the 1960 Oldsmobile were even flatter than those of the 1959 Olds. The grille was broken up into a horizontal grid that was defined by negative space, and the roof described a gracious curve down the rear window pillars that verged on incongruity with the horizontality of the rest of the design.

The power plant for the 1960 Ninety-Eight and the Super Eighty-Eight was a 300-hp, 394-ci (6.5 L) V-8, attached to a Jetaway Hydramatic Drive transmission, while the power plant for the Dynamic Eighty-Eight was a 371-ci (6.1 L) unit. Standard equipment for the Ninety-Eight included some items that were standard on the lower lines and some that were optional on those. All in all, it included a padded dashboard; courtesy lights; a Star-lite headliner; two-speed windshield wipers; chrome roof side moldings; a Safety-Vee steering wheel; turn signals; a Safety-spectrum speedometer with Cruise Control; power steering; power brakes; windshield washers; an electric clock; deep twist carpeting; and a choice of fabric, leather or 'Morocceen' upholstery.

Optional equipment—much of which was optional on the lower lines—included dual exhaust pipes; a heavy duty air filter/engine breather system; a heater/defroster; a deluxe radio; an electric antenna; backup lamps; a park-

ing brake signal lamp; windshield washers; deluxe tri-tone horns; a sideview mirror; power windows; power seats; and 'Fiesta' luggage carrier.

Pontiac, of course, also had its input into the lower-price luxury and family car market with the top-level Bonneville, as well as the lower-level Star Chief and Catalina lines. The Bonneville of 1961 was 209.7 inches in overall length. Its standard features included some items that were also standard on the lower lines, and many that were either optional or unavailable on same.

These standard features included cigarette lighters; sunvisors; two-speed electric windshield wipers; a custom steering wheel; an electric clock; ash trays; foam-padded rear seats; a padded instrument panel; courtesy lights;

and a choice of upholstery materials and special interior accents.

The base Bonneville engine was a 389-ci (6.4 L) V-8 that was rigged for 235 hp if mated to a synchromesh transmission, or 303 hp if mated to an automatic. This compared to the 215/283-hp unit used in the Catalina and Star Chief lines. Bonnevilles were presented in Vista Sedan, hardtop coupe and convertible variants; and a station wagon variant was billed separately as the Bonneville Custom Safari station wagon, which had vertical taillights and special ornamentation. The Catalina also featured station wagon variants, sedans and a convertible, while the Star Chief was strictly a sedan.

The list of options for Bonnevilles and lower-level Pon-

Oldsmobile was, with Buick, one of General Motors' lower-level luxury cars. *Above:* A 1960 Oldsmobile Dynamic Eighty-Eight convertible.

This car offered luxurious size and a 371-ci (6.1 L) V-8 of 240 hp. The top of Oldsmobile's offerings was the Ninety-Eight, which included padded dashboard, power steering, power brakes and a 300-hp, 394-ci (6.5 L) in its list of standard features.

Are they making the turnpikes shorter this year?

Take that next trip in a '61 Plymouth. This Solid Beauty will give you a feeling that roads have never been so smooth, horizons so easy to catch. Everything about this low-price car takes you there in new comfort. It's easy to get in, easy to sit in, easy to see out of. Its quiet one-piece welded Unibody is smoothing the kinks out of the miles. sion (no extra cost) takes practically all the sway and dip out of driving. Plymouth is smoothing the kinks out of the miles. Let your Plymouth dealer show you how.

'61 PLYMOUTH...SOLID BEAUTY

A CHRYSLER ENGINEERED PRODUCT

Ordinary full-size makes could offer performance and luxury as well.

Above: An advertisement featuring Plymouth full-size cars for 1961. The Plymouth Fury was the top-level offering, and was available with engines ranging from a 318-ci (5.2-L) V-8 of 260 hp, to a 413-ci (6.8-L) V-8 of 375 hp.

Then again, there were purer strains of 'muscle cars.' Premier among the early-1960s muscle cars was the powerful Chrysler 300 series, which had dominated American motorsports since the mid-1950s.

Opposite: A 1961 Chrysler 300-G convertible. This sleek and aggressive-looking automobile housed a 375-hp, 413-ci (6.8-L) V-8 as standard equipment, and featured an optional 400-hp version of same.

tiacs that year included Safe-T-Track differential, Tri-power induction (three two-barrel carburetors), air conditioning, electric antenna, power windows, lightweight wheel hubs and brake drums, Cruise Control, heavy-duty springs, tinted glass and more.

The Plymouth Fury was that manufacturer's top-level car at the outset of the 1960s. These cars had wheelbases of 116 inches, and overall lengths of 202 inches, and were like the lower-level Savoy and Belvedere models in that regard, and shared some standard equipment with them.

The 1962 Plymouth Fury, for instance, had standard equipment including aluminum exterior trim inserts; backup lights; an electric clock and power tailgate window (on nine-passenger station wagons). The Sport Fury, however, was the ultimate in the Fury line. This car was offered in two-door hardtop and convertible models. Standard equipment included bucket seats; a center console; full wheel covers; vinyl trim; foam-padded rear seats; and a deluxe steering wheel.

Plymouths of 1961 and 1962 had oddly plain, concave-looking bodies, so the Furies received a third taillight and extended body trim in mid-year 1962. The Sport Furies were distinguished from other Furies by the placement of their signature name ahead of the front wheel well openings and by a strongly segmented grille.

In addition to such intermediate- and full-size offerings from the 'Big Three,' there was also the mid-size Rambler Classic and the luxurious Ambassador, as well as the Studebaker Hawk—a racy-looking mid-size car that had long been widely admired for its sleek good looks.

Then again, there were the truly epochal 'muscle cars,' which seemed a strange combination of near-compact-car size and luxury car engine. They were refined, certainly, to be exactly what most of them were: highway missiles; dragsters; and race cars straight from the factory to the public. Here again is an intersection of autos that were family cars, given one treatment, and were competition machines, given another treatment.

I have explained in the introduction how the 'muscle car' concept came to be, as a hybridization of Detroit production savvy and back-yard garage daring. Even Rambler got into the act, in the late 1960s. The 'muscle car' represented a competition between manufacturers that would last the decade, and would supplant the old hot rodder's 'Chrysler hemi-in-a-1953 Ford' formula for the most part

with machines that were essentially bought direct from the factory.

The 1960 Chrysler 300F, armed with a 375-hp 413 (6.8 L) V-8, won the first six places in the Flying Mile competition at Daytona, attaining a top speed of 145 mph. Chrysler 300Gs of 1961 had the same engine, as did the 1962 300H and the 1963 300J (there was, inexplicably, no 300I), both of which featured improved compression, and registered 380 and 390 hp, respectively.

The heavy-firepower Chryslers (also Dodges and Plymouths) of the early 1960s featured ram induction, wherein the twin four-barrel carburetors sat atop manifolds that had elongated induction tubes that provided a unique vacuum environment that created a better air/fuel mix and 'rammed' the mixture into the cylinders, providing higher horsepower.

Though the 300s of later years eventually saw both the 383-ci (6.3 L) V-8 and the 440-ci (7.2) V-8, the 300's days as a performance car were slowly but surely superseded by its status as an offshoot of the prestigious New Yorker line.

While the Pontiac GTO was perhaps the most well-publicized of the 1960s muscle cars, with a potent publicity machine behind it, an extensive list of options and its oversize engine/small sedan body formula, mention should certainly be made of those old competitors, Chevrolet and Ford, who entered their own sedan 'roadburners' in the lists well before Pontiac did.

The 1961 Chevrolet Impala was offered with optional equipment including a 409-ci (6.7 L) V-8 (actually a truck engine), positraction rear end, dual exhausts and a four-speed transmission, garnering a reputation for itself on the street, but not coming off that impressively at the drag strip. The following years saw the addition of aluminum front fenders and hood among the options. This was more a beefed-up family car than a hair-raising muscle car, but it served enough notice of itself that it was acclaimed in at least one top-40 song, the Beach Boys' 'Giddyup 409.'

Also, the advent of the 327-ci (5.4 L) V-8 for Chevrolet Corvettes around the turn of the decade caused the Corvette to begin acquiring a reputation for itself. The first really bold step was yet to come, however.

Meanwhile, Ford was busy stuffing its 352-ci (5.8 L) engine into the Galaxie model cars. This engine came in several versions, with 235, 300 and 360 hp—the latter of

Above: A 1961 Chevrolet Corvette. This sporty little car was beginning to acquire a 'muscle car reputation' at the outset of the 1960s. Its standard engine was a 230-hp, 283-ci (4.7-L) V-8, with optional performance treatments to boost its power output up to 315 hp.

Opposite: A 1961 Oldsmobile Dynamic Eighty-Eight Holiday Coupe. Its aggressive styling was meant to give it a 'performance car' look, and its 394-ci (6.5-L) V-8 was available in a 325-hp version.

which was the street emulation of the NASCAR engines with which such notable drivers as 'Fireball' Roberts, Dan Gurney, Norm Nelson, Parnelli Jones, AJ Foyt, Fred Lorenzen and Cale Yarborough created track legends based on Ford performance.

Then again, there existed the 'luxury muscle cars' of which I speak in the first chapter of this text. While these 'bruisers in gentlefolk's clothes' would never be able to surpass the soon-to-come AC Ford Cobra or the 'hemi 'Cuda,' they delivered what was promised by their manufacturers: they would allow their passengers get where they wanted to go with power and speed to spare, in an atmosphere of sporty styling and luxury.

The first of these was Ford Motor Company's Thunder-

bird, which began as a well-appointed and potent little two-seater back in 1955. The 'T-Bird' effectively evoked the fast and spiffy 'gentleman's roadsters' of the 1920s. It was in a class by itself in the 1950s.

However, the Thunderbird grew from its original two-seat configuration, 102-inch wheelbase and 175.3-inch overall length to a four-seat configuration, 119 inches and 205.32 inches, respectively, in 1958—a change that was to proclaim a point of no return. The Thunderbird's size would hover around those marks for the rest of the decade, and would *never* revert to its original size. This was partly attributable to the fact that Ford needed a true lower-level luxury car to round out its model portfolio. Since it had become clear that the Corvette and the Thunderbird were

not going to be direct competitors, the Thunderbird was then free to fulfill other of Ford's competitive obligations.

Hence, the Thunderbird became a larger version of itself—once a luxury muscle car, always a luxury muscle car. This concept was to spawn its own competitors in the 1960s: first, the Buick Riviera was wheeled out the factory gates to do battle in this market segment; and then Oldsmobile pulled a real coup with the front-wheel-drive Toronado.

The Thunderbird for 1960 was offered in two types: a two-door coupe and a two-door convertible. This car was the last of the 'square birds,' so-called because of their 1958 Galaxie-inspired front end and squared-off rear end. The 1960 Thunderbirds were discernable from their 1958–59 brethren by the use of three (as opposed to the earlier models' two) taillights per side. Standard equipment included vinyl bucket seats separated by a console, and instrument panel with white-faced gauges.

The standard power train was a 300-hp, 352-ci (5.8 L) V-8 with a three-speed manual transmission. An optional, 350-hp, 430-ci (seven L) V-8 was available—strictly with a Cruise-O-Matic automatic transmission. The luxury of the 1960 Thunderbird was provided in part through a long list of convenience options, including power steering; power brakes; power windows; a Cruise-O-Matic transmission; overdrive for the standard transmission; a radio and antenna; a heater; an air conditioner; tinted glass; four-way power seats; sideview mirrors on both sides; backup lights; windshield washers; rear fender shields; front seat belts; a leather interior; underseal; a heavy-duty battery; two-tone paint; and a sun roof for the hard top. The hardtop was offered for a $3755 base factory price, and the convertible was offered for $4222.

The year 1961 saw a new Thunderbird with the bullet-nose profile that the Ford designers had given the car that year. Also, standard equipment included a 300-hp, 390-ci (6.4 L) V-8 with Cruise-O-Matic transmission; power steering; and power brakes. Additional engine options on the 390 offered high-compression 375- and 401-hp versions that were considered more competition engines than street engines, and were more likely, despite their 'Thunderbird Special' designation, to turn up under the hood of a Galaxie than under the engine bonnet of a 'T-bird.' The factory price of a 1961 Thunderbird hardtop coupe was $4170, while the convertible variant cost $4637.

Above: A 1960 Ford Galaxie 500 Starliner—one of the best Ford body designs, ever. It was available with 352-ci (5.8 L) V-8s of 235, 300 or 360 hp, and optional differential ratios to maximize such power.

A prime example of the early-1960s luxury muscle car was the Ford Thunderbird—a sleek paean to Ford styling.

Opposite: A 1962 Ford Thunderbird two-door hardtop coupe. *At right:* A taillight view of a 1962 Thunderbird. This car's engine options included 300- and 340-hp versions of Ford's 390-ci (6.4-L) V-8. Also available for Ford products of that year was a 406-ci V-8 of 405 hp.

THE ASCENDANT DECADE

Perhaps it was the youthful appeal of President John F Kennedy, or perhaps it was a shift in the Jet Stream, but the 1960s did not take long to establish a direction—and that direction was toward an increasing emphasis on youth and the young, on idealistic notions and social change. For automobiles, this meant a growing mutability.

For instance, the Studebaker Lark was both an economy car and a car that could be transformed, with suitable option choices, into a far different machine—as is evidenced by the four-speed floor-shift transmission that was available on 289-ci (4.7 L) V-8 versions of the 1962 Lark Daytona.

Also that year, a styling change produced a sleeker look and added nearly 10 inches to the Lark's overall length. The 112-hp six would reign as the king of economy at Studebaker, and was usually linked to a three-speed manual transmission for maximum gas-saving effect. The Larks were to change again in 1964, with wheelbases that went from 190 inches for two-door sedans to 194 inches for four-door sedans.

The Chevrolet Corvairs of 1962 saw the expansion of the Monza line to include a convertible and a station wagon; as well as the addition to the Corvair line of the Monza Spyder, which was designed to represent the peak of Corvair performance, with a more powerful engine, and a four-speed transmission.

This was also the year that Chevrolet installed a much stiffer handling package in the Corvair. Complaints that the car was a bit hard to handle had started mounting to a background din. In wet conditions, or in turns at speed, the rear end wanted to break loose and swing around to the front, and the car had pronounced oversteer in general.

Questions were raised about the chassis design. This led Chevrolet to install a transverse compensator spring, to help correct a problem with the rear wheels, which tended to tuck under, adding to the car's skitterish handling.

The engine was another point of contention. Corvairs were powered by a 'pancake' six-cylinder that, oddly, had bushings instead of main bearings, and was made of aluminum. The theory went that, with plenty of oil, the bushing would last as long as a bearing, but this was not so.

Options were the name of the game in the early 1960s. *At right:* **An inside view of a 1963 Ford Galaxie 500 XL—revealing, among other things, Ford's optional Selectaire air conditioning system.**
The Galaxie 500 XL was the top-of-the-line Ford. Ford presented a special fastback roof for the Galaxie 500 in late 1963, and dubbed the design a '1963 and one-half' model. The fastback was a hit, proving that the sloping roof was 'in.'
Opposite: A 1964 Galaxie 500 XL, complete with fastback roof. Note the '390' engine designation badge just behind the front wheel well.

Above: An advertisement for the 1961 Corvair line. The car was not popular at first, but came to have a belated romantic appeal, due to its unusual design and its much-admired body styling.

Despite the claims that this advertisement makes, driving the Corvair could be a terrifying experience for the uninitiated—and was unpredictable even for the experienced.

At right: A promotional photo of the 1962 Corvair Monza convertible, which was designed to enhance the Corvair's image as a sports car.

This page: **Two views of a 1962 Chevrolet Impala sedan—the top-of-the line Chevrolet. It could be bought as an upscale family car, with a mild version of the 283-ci (4.7 L) V-8 as a standard engine—or as a fire-breathing muscle car, with options up to a 409-hp, 409-ci (6.7 L) V-8.**

Since the Impala was built around the same basic body as the lower-priced Bel Air and Biscayne models, it was possible to buy a cheaper car that emulated the Impala's good looks—and at the same time enjoy the economy of a six-cylinder power plant, if one so chose.

These engines suffered early burnout when the main bushings wore down, and the aluminum block contributed to overheating. Another liability was that the air-cooled 140-ci (2.2 L) Corvair six was a much larger engine than the tiny Volkswagen air-cooled four.

It therefore was in need of a better air-ducting system to suit its cooling needs. This it had, when the car was in motion. Stuck in traffic, though, it was a different story, especially with the station wagon variants.

The design of the Corvair wagons was at first considered a triumph. It seemed ingenious that Chevrolet could shoehorn a flat-six engine in a station wagon and still allow for rear entry. The design soon revealed its own air-ducting inadequacy: quite simply, the station wagon deck was in the way. For all of the bravura attached to the Corvair—racing accessories became available in later years—it

was not a car, until very late in its career, to live up to the advertising hype.

Options for the 1962 Corvair included a choice of three- or four-speed manual transmission, as well as a two-speed automatic. Two engine options, 80-hp (on Standard and Deluxe models) or 95-hp (on Monza models), were also offered.

The year 1964 saw much the same Corvair model lineup as 1962, except that Series 500 and 700 offerings were severely cut back to a club coupe and a sedan, respectively.

Chevrolet introduced its Chevelle in 1964, as a filler for the gap between its full-size cars and the Chevy II. The Chevelle never really was a compact, fitting more into the intermediate range than into the announced 'senior compact' status that Chevrolet granted it.

Chevelles were offered as sedans, convertibles and station wagons—and in this last capacity were a real boon to the family car market. They were reasonably compact, but, at 198.8 inches long, were large enough to handle almost any hauling chore the average family of the time might have had. That it was to achieve status as a muscle car is discussed elsewhere in this text.

The Falcon version of the famed Country Squire station wagon appeared in 1962, complete with simulated wooden body panels. Also, two complete lines of trim standard were established, with the Standard and Deluxe Falcons being offered as two levels.

Bolder use of chrome, and the establishment of two-door hardtop and convertible models were big Falcon news for 1963. Also, Ford decided to give the Falcon Futura line a bit more punch by the introduction of the Futura Sprint model. Sprints were offered as either two-door coupes or convertibles, with a 260-ci (4.3 L) Ford V-8 of 164 hp for power.

You could buy a brand-new Sprint coupe from the factory for $2603, while the convertible cost just $200 more.

Falcon got a more angular, racier-looking body for 1964, and heavier concentration was focused on the Futura line. Standard Falcons offered only two- and four-door sedans, while station wagons became a separate Falcon line and the Futura line offered nine variants—including Sports models and, of course, the new hot seller, the Sprint convertible and coupe. Falcon overall lengths remained roughly the same as for those first-year Falcons, at approx-

imately 181 inches for passenger cars and 189 inches for station wagons.

Meanwhile, Ford had made their base-level, full-size Fairlane an intermediate in 1962, with an overall length of 197.6 inches. This first year, they were available only as two- and four-door sedans, but station wagons and coupes appeared in 1963, adding range to this new Ford entry into the family car market. The Fairlane, like its opposite number, the Chevelle, was to make its mark as a muscle car as well—as I discuss elsewhere.

Round taillights made their appearance on the Mercury Comets of 1962, and this was carried over to the 1963 Comet line. The stock transmission was a three-speed standard, and options included a four-speed standard and three-speed Mercomatic automatic units. Power plant options included the same 101-hp, 260-ci (4.3 L) V-8 that powered the Falcon Futura Sprints.

Comets were yet further examples of family cars that could be transformed into pavement burning projectiles with the choice of certain options. These smallest Mercurys were given a squared-off look for 1964. The stock engine was the 170-ci (2.7 L) six. A new model was introduced, the Caliente, which was advertised as Comet's sporty variant. With upper-level trim, padded dash, walnut accents and deep carpeting, the Calientes were very popular.

However, Mercury's offering for the compact car horsepower wars was the Comet Cyclone—stock with bucket seats, console and 289-ci (4.7 L) V-8 of 210 hp, with an optional treatment giving it 271 hp. The optional four-speed standard transmission was the way to go with the Cyclone. As cited in my discussion on muscle cars, Mercury backed several Cyclones for the drag strip, equipping them with decidedly non-street running gear.

The Mercury Meteor, offered in sedan and station wagon models, was Mercury's entrant into the mid-size family car market.

In 1963, Plymouth Valiants received a squared-off body treatment with traditional notchback styling. They were sprightly-looking little cars, and included the V-100 and V-200 series, as well as the Signet line—which this year had hardtop and convertible models, both with bucket seats. The Signets were the premium-price Valiants, and even at that, a hardtop cost $2230 from the factory, and a convertible cost $2454.

Above: **A 1963 Falcon Futura Sprint convertible. As compared with the Falcons pictured on pages 18–19, this design evidences Ford's then-increasing interest in offering a car that had both economy and sportiness. With an optional 260-ci (4.3-L) V-8, it also had some power.**

As one moved into the mid-size Fords, like the 1964 Fairlane 500 coupe *at left*, the aura of comparative roominess also evoked thought of a decision: 'six or V-8?' The V-8s included 260-ci (4.3 L) and 289-ci (4.7 L) units.

For 1964, Valiants got a minor facelift, including the positioning of vertical, rectangular taillights on the ends of the rear fenders. Also, a 180-hp, 273-ci (4.4 L) V-8 became an option. An interesting spinoff of the Valiant was the fastback Barracuda, which I discuss more fully as a muscle car. The Barracuda, meant as a direct competitor for the Ford Mustang, had the same engine and transmission options as the Valiant.

The Dodge Dart was downsized to compact dimensions in 1963. With an overall length of 195.9 inches for sedan bodies and 190.2 inches for station wagons, it was one of the larger compacts. It was a nicely styled car, with a sporty, forward-looking appeal.

Three trim levels—Dart 170, Dart 270 and Dart GT—existed, with a station wagon and two- and four-door sedans available in the 170 series; the same plus a convertible in the 270 series; and two-door hardtop and convertible available for the GT. Engine offerings were the same as for the Lancers of the previous year.

In 1964, a 180-hp, 273-ci (4.4 L) V-8 was added to the engine options for the Dodge Dart. This was a very popular package, and, with a transmission option range like that of the Plymouth Valiant, was a versatile one as well.

Buick offered a 135-hp, 198-ci (3.2 L) V-6, as well as the aluminum V-8 for its Specials of 1962. Oldsmobile stayed with the V-8 exclusively, going deeper into performance with a turbocharged Jetfire Coupe producing 215 hp with the little V-8, which is also discussed elsewhere in this text.

The Buick Skylark, like its lower-priced Special brethren, added a convertible model that year, as did the Standard and Deluxe F-85s.

The Pontiac Tempest wasn't much changed for 1962, except that a convertible model was added to the line. In 1963, Tempests began their inflation to 'senior compact' status, which meant that the wheelbase (112 inches) stayed the same, while the overall length grew to 194.3 inches. The top-of-the-line engine option was a 326-ci (5.3 L) V-8.

The Tempest grew again to an intermediate-size 203 inches in 1964. It also was given a standard drivetrain, and a base-level six-cylinder power plant. Of its most famous option package, however, please see the commentary on the GTO.

Chevrolet kept up its end of General Motors sales by offering an alternate to their Corvair—the more conven-

Opposite, above: A 1963 Plymouth Valiant Signet convertible. The Signet was the highest Valiant trim level. Below: A 1964 Plymouth Barracuda. Note the basic body styling it shares with the Valiant just discussed. Opposite, below: A 1964 Dodge Dart. The Dart took

over as Dodge's compact line in 1963, when the company dropped the Lancer, a Valiant look-alike. Buyers of 1974 Valiant, Dart and Barracuda models could choose one of two sixes or a small-block V-8 to power their spritely-looking compact cars.

tional Chevy II, in 1963. This was a pleasingly-proportioned car of 183 inches overall length (187.4 inches for station wagons).

Four- and two-door sedans, plus two-door station wagons were offered, while the 400 Series Chevy IIs offered two-door sedan, sport coupe and convertible models, plus four-door station wagon and sedan models.

The engines were a four-cylinder of 90 hp and 153.3 cubic (2.5 L) inches, and a six-cylinder of 120 hp and 194.4-aci (3.1 L). Also, there was an option that offered either a 283 (4.7 L) or a 327-ci (5.4 L) V-8.

For 1963, the Chevy II had the same basic styling, and offered the same models, except for the two-door sedan in the 400 Series. The Super Sport option—basically a higher trim level—was also offered.

A minor body-style alteration was performed for the year 1964, and the intermediate-price 300 Series was eliminated. Also, the Nova Super Sport, a two-door sport coupe, was added above the 400 Series.

Of course, 1964 saw the advent of the car that outsold them all: the Ford Mustang. Of this famous vehicle, I also talk extensively in the discussion of 'muscle cars' below. That the Mustang was a superb runabout and generally sprightly little compact was also part of its charm. The Mustang sold one million units in its first two years.

With an overall length of 181.6 inches, it was a handy, fairly economical little compact car. Of course, you could also order your Mustang in a form that would burn up the dragstrip. The place to make that decision was at your friendly Ford dealer, who would gladly help you select the Mustang that suited your needs.

In the realm of luxury, the Chrysler Crown Imperial was not offered in 1962, which was the same year that saw the tailfins on other Imperials all but disappear.

The Crown Imperial was, however, offered in 1963, with a price tag of $18,500. This may seem excruciatingly high compared to the $9939 asked for the Cadillac Fleetwood limousine of that same year, but bear in mind that these are base prices. Chrysler's Crown Imperial was custom-built by the legendary Ghia coachbuilding firm of Italy, and almost every optional feature on the Chrysler list was a *standard item* for the Crown Imperial—it was a car with 'all the toys and whistles' built in.

Still, when one considers that the factory price for middle-range cars like the Chevrolet Impala and the

Dodge Polara hovered around $3000, $18,000 for any car, no matter how fine, was an enormous amount of money.

In 1964, Chrysler's entire Imperial line was restyled with a treatment very similar to that given the Lincoln Continentals of the 1960s. This trim, boxy look was just right for luxury cars, and Chrysler Corporation felt obliged to alter it very little, adding a simulated spare tire bulge on the rear of the deck lid, and giving the rear quarter panels a slight, rakish tilt to the fore.

Cadillac believed in presenting the buyer with an excellent base-level car, and as one rose up the price scale, things simply got more and more luxurious. As the 1960s progressed, Cadillac styling integrated the famous tailfins into the dorsal surfaces of the rear fenders, and the grillework receded between jutting front fender edges.

This page: Two views of a 1963 Chevy II Nova SS sport coupe. The Chevy II offered both four- and six-cylinder models, while the top-level Nova was strictly a six-cylinder car—unless the Nova buyer chose an optional 283-ci (4.7 L) or 327-ci (5.4 L) V-8.

Opposite: A 1962 Pontiac Tempest LeMans convertible. The Tempest was offered that year with an optional aluminum-block V-8 of 215 ci (3.5 L)—an engine also used in the Oldsmobile F-85 of that year.

Opposite: A 1963 Cadillac Series 6200 convertible. Compare this with earlier Cadillacs (please see pages 22–24).

Power brakes and power steering, plus a record-breaking list of 163 options, made even this low-level Cadillac a very luxurious car.

Below: A 1964 Rambler Classic 550 four-door sedan. While the Classic was the mid-range Rambler line—between the compact American and the upscale Ambassador—the 550 was the lowest Classic trim level, with the 660 and 770 representing the 'next steps up.'

The Lincoln Continental, like the Cadillac, also offered an element of prestige that sometimes eluded the Imperial (being, as the Imperial was, the product of the third-ranked automaker in the US, whereas the 'competition' were produced by the 'top two').

As for lower-priced luxury and other full-size cars of the early 1960s, the offerings were many and varied. Beginning with the Studebaker Hawk, an intermediate, and the four-door Larks that were as close to full-size cars as that company got in the early 1960s; and the Rambler Classic and the top-of-the-line Ambassador—not to forget the Checker cars that were but rarely seen outside of taxicab duty—America offered the consumer a vast array of designs.

Among these, the Buick Electra was actually upstaged by the appearance of the sporty-looking Buick Riviera of 1963. Here was a Buick that was both plush and sporty, and it was, in a sense, an outgrowth of the Electra line.

However, even though Rivieras tended to top the Buick price range, at a factory price of $4333 for the only model offered, a four-passenger coupe, the Electra had the heft, shall I say, of a truly luxurious car, with a 4284-pound

weight for the four-passenger hardtop, a 126-inch wheelbase and an overall length of 221.6 inches.

By comparison, the first-year Riviera weighed 3998 pounds, and had a 117-inch wheelbase and an overall length of 208 inches. Please see the commentary on the Buick Riviera in my discussion of luxury muscle cars.

The Le Sabre that year was represented by two- and four-door sedan and hardtop models, while the Invicta series offered two- and four-door hardtop models, as well as a convertible and six- and eight-passenger station wagon models.

The large, top-level Chryslers lost their fins in 1962, though they had gained over-and-under quad headlights that were set at an angle, giving the front ends of the cars a 'cat's eyes' look.

This year also saw the introduction of a confusingly-designated Sport Series 300, a lower-level car that was outwardly distinguishable from the upper-level 300H by its less bold grille, its inclusion of a four-door hardtop among its types (the 300 Series had not, to that point, done so) and the absence of the '300H' insignia on the trunk lid.

The year 1963 saw the introduction of the somewhat boxy, sloping hood and decklid look that was a Chrysler classic for two short years. By contrast, the 1965 New Yorker offered a more straightforward look, with slab sides that were subtly broken by lengthwise curves, and a tasteful, sloping-windshield-and-rear-window cockpit.

The Chrysler Town & Country station wagon models were attached to the base-level Newport series, which also featured a sedan, a convertible and two hardtops. Upper-level Town & Country station wagons were offered through the New Yorker series.

Long considered to be Ford Motor Company's producer of cars for those who wanted something just a touch more classy than a Ford, Mercury brought out its first true lower-level luxury car of the 1960s with the Park Lane of 1964, which carried on an honorable tradition handed down from the Mercury Monterey.

Oldsmobile styling moved into a pleasing simplicity that at once echoed the sleek Pontiacs and the satisfyingly blunt Lincoln Continentals of the time. By 1964, Oldsmobile had adopted a number of low- and mid-range cars to supplement their Eighty-Eight and Ninety-Eight offerings. Among these were the Starfire, the Vista Cruiser and the Cutlass.

The Vista Cruiser represented a line of station wagons that had a stepdown roof into which was fitted a sheet of glass, so that rear-seat passengers could view the forward scenery nearly as well as those in the front seats.

However, the Ninety-Eight was to remain at the top of the Oldsmobile luxury market—but had a companion or two in that exalted position as the years rolled on.

In 1963, Plymouth undertook a restyling, and arrived at the wedge-like look that was to echo through the Plymouth full-size lines for the rest of the decade.

The base engine for the Plymouth Sport Fury was a 318-ci (5.2 L) V-8 of 230 hp. Optional engines included a 383-ci (6.3 L) 'Golden Commando' V-8 of a reputed 410 hp. Power brakes, power steering, air conditioning, cigar lighter, tinted glass, padded dashboard, windshield washers and other convenience items were included among available options. The factory base price for a 1962 Sport Fury convertible was $3082. This model is now considered a collector's item.

Echoing the sleek lines of the Sport Fury were Plymouth's lesser-expensive full-size models, the Savoy, the Belvedere and the Fury proper. Savoys were available only as sedans and station wagons, while the Belvedere offered sedan, station wagon and hardtop coupe models.

For 1964, Pontiac's Bonneville was 220 inches in overall length. It was distinguished by having ribbed rocker panel molding, front and rear fender extensions, deluxe wheel covers, deluxe steering wheel, two-speed windshield wipers, electronic clock, courtesy lamps, padded dashboard and foam-padded rear seats. The base engine was a 389 (6.4 L) V-8 with similar horsepower ratings to those cited elsewhere in this text for 1961.

There was also a Grand Prix model, strictly a sports coupe, that was built on the Catalina chassis, and featured concave rear windows; taillight grilles; wood-grain interior trim; dual exhausts; bucket seats; a center console; and front foam seat cushions. The base V-8 was the same as that used for the Bonneville.

Meanwhile, the lower-level full-size Pontiacs included the Catalina and Star Chief lines, both of which offered sedans, with the lower-level Catalina also offering sport coupe, convertible and station wagon configurations.

In 1963, the restyled Corvette splashed upon the scene as the Corvette Stingray, creating ripples throughout the auto industry. It was the sleekest American car to have been introduced since Ford Motor Company's incredible 1956–57 Continental Mark II.

Way back in 1959, General Motors stylist Bill Mitchell had crafted a very futuristic, streamlined body for a Corvette SS frame and entered the car, named the *Sting Ray*, in the President's Cup race at Marlboro Raceway in Maryland. The car placed fourth in that race, and after more racing, was placed on the auto show circuit in 1961.

The production Stingray emerged shortly thereafter, with many of its progenitor's racing features incorporated—to the delight of anxious Stingray customers. The

Vista-Cruiser by OLDSMOBILE

Stingray was a revolutionary design, bigger than most sports cars, and was endowed with the street car muscle that Detroit best knew how to provide—it was a drag racing road machine, one of the hybrids that America produces from time to time to the astonishment of the world at large.

The car featured a fully independent suspension, a fuel-injected 360-hp, 327-ci (5.4 L) engine and both convertible and coupe models. (The only Stingray coupe to feature the now-classic split rear window was the 1963 model.)

In 1963, Chevrolet introduced its full-competition 427-ci (6.9 L) engine as an option for its conventional sedans—a fact that made that engine NASCAR-legal, and caused Ford and Chrysler Corporation many nasty surprises on the stock car circuit.

The street version was actually a 'stroked' 409 (6.7 L) (ie, the length of piston travel in the cylinder was increased to increase the engine's volume to 427 ci [6.9 L]). This was offered with a dual-exhaust, four-speed standard transmission and heavy duty rearend package for the street or strip, in the famed 'Z-II' option package for the Impala Sport Coupe.

Above: A 1962 Plymouth Belvedere four-door sedan. This was the last year for the unusual styling that full-size Plymouths were given in 1961. Wedge-like bodies would dominate Plymouths of the later 1960s (please see pages 78–79).

The base engine for this car was a choice of 'old standby' Plymouth hardware: a 225-ci (3.6 L) slant six, or a 318-ci V-8. The top option was a 383-ci (6.3 L) V-8.

Chevrolet caused a sensation with the introduction of the restyled Corvette for 1963. Aptly called the 'Stingray,' this was one of the sleekest American autos to that date.

The base engine was a 327-ci (5.4 L), 250-hp V-8, and performance options upped this output to a maximum of 360 hp. *Below:* A rear view of a 1963 Corvette Stingray fastback coupe. *Opposite:* A 1963 Stingray convertible, with custom wheels.

At left: An elegant 1964 Pontiac Bonneville Club de Mer convertible. The standard engine was a 389-ci (6.4 L) V-8, with a 421-ci (6.9-L) V-8 as an option. The well-proportioned Pontiac body style was much emulated by other carmakers in the 1960s.

The other Chevrolet 427 (6.9 L) was the so-called NASCAR 'mystery' engine, with its combustion chambers located in its heads, and with valves that were staggered, giving later 396-ci (6.5 L) and 454-ci (7.4 L) variants on this engine the nickname 'porcupine,' 'rat motor' and so forth, in honor of the bristling appearance of its valve arrangement.

The new 'mystery' engine dominated NASCAR for one year, until Chrysler Corporation came out with its ground-shaking 426 (6.9 L) hemi. The hemi had a better 'top end' than the 'mystery' engine, but the horsepower wars did not end there. As is customary in the auto industry, performance advances appear on the racetrack first, and then, on the street.

Ford, not to be outdone by General Motors, entered their 1963 fastback Galaxie into the lists with optional dual exhausts, four speed transmission and a slightly upgraded 390-ci (6.4 L) engine. This, again, was a full-size car, and served to wet the tastebuds of the youth market. For those whose tastes ran to the pungent, the 427 (6.9 L) Thunderbird V-8 was a real attention-getter in two versions of 410 and 425 hp, and was also available in the street Galaxie.

Ford made a strong appearance on the NASCAR ovals with these engines. Then again, rumors of the Shelby Cobra had reached some ears, and the Corvette was busy making its reputation. The era of the 1960s muscle car was truly coming into prominence.

In fact, Ford launched a 'Total Performance' assault on the automotive world at large. Projects such as that involving 427-ci (6.9 L) engines and the 1964 mid-size Fairlanes were making news at the drag strip. The Fairlanes, running under the tribal name of 'Thunderbolt,' dominated the A/Stock class in 1964, trouncing the big Chevrolets.

It was interesting to see these cars—usually encountered as understated family sedans or station wagons—sprinting out over the drag strip starting lines at velocities that would be ludicrous and cartoon-like in their exaggerated intensity, if seen on the average street.

Impressive as the other muscle cars of the era were, there was one car that could beat them all. It existed in a class by itself. This car, which first appeared in 1962, still holds the title as the fastest-accelerating production car in the world. It was the Ford AC Cobra, which seemed a small but rather stocky sportscar at first glance, until it left you in the dust with a roar, accelerating from 0 to 60 mph in under four seconds, and 0 to 100 mph in 8.6 seconds.

The Cobra began as an inspiration for Carroll Shelby, a successful American race car driver of international caliber who was forced to quit racing by a heart condition. In his years as a driver, he had noticed that the European cars could easily outhandle American cars, but could in no way out-accelerate America's big V-8s. He resolved to combine the two advantages in one car.

His choice of body and chassis was that of the Ace, manufactured by the AC company of Thames Ditton, England. Shelby's engines were supplied by the Ford Motor Company. The first power plant he installed in the AC carbody was a 260-ci (4.3 L) Ford V-8. This went into the first 75 Cobras, which were availed to the public via Ford dealerships—as were most Cobras, even including the 427-ci (6.9 L) rockets that culminated the lineage.

Then Ford offered Shelby the upscale 289-ci (4.7 L) V-8, and this became the power center of the Cobra. As with all modifications and improvements made down through the years, many Cobra owners brought their hot little machines back to the manufacturer for retrofitting.

There was an ulterior motive on Shelby's part. He had developed the car to 'blow Ferrari's ass off' and therefore, the Cobras went racing, with Ford Motor Company as a backer. They were virtually unbeatable, and thrashed not only the Ferraris, but also their closest domestic competitor, the brand-new Corvette Stingrays.

General Motors did not take kindly to this, and decided to get even. In December of 1963, the Cobras descended on Nassau for the annual Speed Week races there, which featured all-out competition of the 'run what you brung' school. Chevrolet worked up a flock of Grand Sport Corvettes, which were not legal for the SCCA and FIA events in which Corvettes normally met Cobras, but at Nassau, that didn't matter. These Grand Sports were super-lightweight race cars with 377-ci (6.1 L) all-aluminum V-8s of 480 hp. They left the Cobras in the dust.

That led Ken Miles, Cobra's head driver, to stuff a full-competition Ford 427-ci (6.9 L) V-8 into a Cobra chassis. This car was extremely fast and very dangerous to drive, as the old AC leaf-spring suspension was not up to the torque and weight of the big V-8. The car lapped the competition but fell apart in its first race.

Opposite: **A 1964 Ford Galaxie 500 XL, caught in a moment of time at the Ford test track in Dearborn, Michigan. The 500 XL had a 427-ci (6.9-L) V-8 as a top engine option—though the optional 390-ci (6.4 L) power plant was more within the needs of most car owners. The 427 was backed by a four-speed standard transmission.**

Below: **A 1963 Galaxie 500 XL convertible. Convertibles were glamorous, and allowed their owners to show off the plush interiors of such upscale cars as the 500 XLs. They were not especially desirable as muscle cars, however, as the lack of a substantial top required an extra-heavy frame underneath, meaning extra weight.**

The second Miles 'special' featured an all-aluminum 390-ci (6.4 L) Ford V-8 with 450 hp, in a Cobra that weighed only 1850 pounds, with a beefed-up chassis. In the 1964 meet at Nassau, Miles left the Grand Sport Corvettes in the dust. Even though this car failed to finish the race, the way of the future was clear.

These developments worked in concert with stiffening competition to wreak an epochal change in America's hottest sportscar. It happened that Ferrari was working toward sufficient production to qualify the super-potent 250 LM for FIA competition, and Chevrolet revealed its plans to install the potent 396-ci (6.5 L) version of their 'mystery' engine in the Corvette—both of which events would make things all too hot for the existing 289 (4.7 L) V-8-powered Cobras in SCCA and FIA competition.

This prompted a move on the part of Ford to offer Shelby and company their 427 (6.9 L) NASCAR special engines, and with the replacement of the old AC Ace leaf spring suspension with an entirely redesigned coil spring suspension and framework, the Cobras were now fire-breathing roadeaters that were more than a match for the competition.

The bodies of these cars had fender flares to give an additional lateral berth for the fat competition tires. Side-pipes, a competition Cobra trademark, added to the intimidating presence of the cars. (Soon enough, street Corvettes were wearing sidepipes, too.) In competition trim, these 427 (6.9 L) Cobras weighed approximately 2300 pounds.

Officially known as the Cobra II, these big-block Cobras were thereafter colloquially called '427 Cobras.' The competition cars exclusively used the Ford NASCAR 427 (6.9 L) engines, which featured direct main bearing oil feed, while many of the street cars were powered by the lower-performance Ford 428-ci (seven L) V-8, a passenger

At left: This was the 289-ci (4.7-L) version of the king of the muscle cars, the Shelby AC Ford Cobra. This little car's 427-ci (6.9-L) descendants would dominate several class categories at sports car tracks and drag strips throughout the mid-to-late 1960s. Unlike many muscle cars, the Cobra did not easily double as a grocery-getter.

Habit-breaker... for people who've been buying the same low-priced make time after time after time

Pontiac's answer to the perennial search for a good, low-priced car was the restyled Tempest of 1964. This year, the former compact had grown into a medium-size car, but still lured economy customers with its base-level six-cylinder engine.

Above: An advertisement for Pontiac's 1964 Tempest.

Pontiac's answer to the demands of the youth market for a less-than-full-size car with an inordinate amount of power was the 1964 Tempest LeMans GTO.

While the initials 'GTO' indicated a performance option package, the public came to think of 'a GTO' as a distinct kind of car.

Opposite: A 1964 Pontiac Tempest LeMans GTO coupe. A 389-ci (6.4 L) V-8 was the heart of the GTO, and the three-two-barrel carburetor setup that produced 348 hp was a further option.

car engine that still gave plenty of punch to the street Cobras.

Meanwhile, Chrysler Corporation's hot engines for 1963 and 1964 were the 426-ci (6.9 L) Dodge Ramcharger and Plymouth Superstock engine options, with either one or two four-barrel carburetors, rated at 410 and 425 hp, respectively. These featured the highly successful 'Ramcharger' manifolds that had induction tubes in a crossover configuration that gave extra potency to the dual four-barrel carburetors they carried.

This system had been a Chrysler Corporation option on their 413-ci (6.8 L) Ramcharger V-8s since 1961. The 426 (6.9 L) Ramcharger engines were purveyed through Chrysler's Dodge and Plymouth lines.

Drag racing teams like Michigan's Ramchargers ran their candy-striped Polaras roughshod over the competition. However, the 426 (6.9 L) Ramcharger and Super-stock engines, featuring wedge-shaped combustion chambers, were not doing so well on the NASCAR circuit, and this prompted Chrysler Corporation to reprise their hemispherical combustion chamber engine of the 1950s. The new 'hemi' had 426 ci (6.9 L), solid lifters and was generally a much less 'soft' engine than had been the old hemi, which was discontinued in 1958.

However, if the hemi were to be legal for NASCAR competition, it would have to be offered as optional equipment for street automobiles—even if it were a 'competition only' option. Therefore, the year 1964 saw Chrysler Corporation offering, way down on their engine options list, a package that included both the Dodge Hemi-Charger (Plymouth Super Commando) and the Dodge Hemi-Charger Eight-Barrel (also Plymouth Super Commando) engines.

Studebaker, although a dying company in the 1960s, had long had a cult of devotees built up around their rakish Hawk coupes. In 1962, Studebaker unveiled a huge surprise in the even more sleek Avanti—on the very brink of the company's demise.

The Avanti's elegant European-inspired lines were the product of the design studios of Raymond Loewy. To call it a muscle car would be to belie the subtlety of its effect: the Avanti seemed to glide past, at whatever speed, like a thing from the future.

Oldsmobile, as well, wanted a share of the performance market. This company had been a force in stock car competition in the mid-1950s, and its various overhead valve V-8s had shown up at the drag strip in one guise or another for years. As of the early 1960s, however, Oldsmobile was not really thought of as a performance manufacturer that one would necessarily mention in the same breath with Ford, Chevrolet or Chrysler products.

Even so, Oldsmobile had its bid in early with the 1962 F-85, powered by the 215-ci (3.5 L) aluminum-block V-8 that I have previously discussed. With its optional 'Jetfire' turbocharger, this little engine would put out 215 hp.

While the F-85 was a good idea, the aluminum V-8 had its share of problems, even though it was used, highly modified, in a Mickey Thompson Indianapolis car, and was featured in at least one lower-class dragster, with a radical cam, high-compression pistons and fuel injectors.

Not to be outdone, the Buick pursuit of performance was represented in part by the Wildcat in 1963. This car had a 340-hp, 401-ci (6.6 L) engine, custom-styled wheels and a variety of performance options. The other part of Buick's performance program appeared in 1963. This was the beautiful new Buick luxury muscle car, the Riviera, which I discuss elsewhere in this chapter.

Pontiac, of course, entered the 1960s with a strong contender in the epochal 1964 GTO, going straight for the high-performance youth market with an all-out offering of street racing accessories.

The GTO program got its start when a General Motors edict to Pontiac in 1963 said 'no more racing components—we're not in that business!' Pontiac sought a new angle to keep their sales going, and advertising man Jim Wangers and John De Lorean went to Pontiac engineer Peter Estes with a plan to put a big-block Pontiac 389 (6.4 L) in the Tempest—which was the smallest Pontiac.

This package, to be called the Tempest GTO, was tendered as merely a selection of options—a 389-ci (6.4 L) V-8 with either a single four-barrel or three two-barrel carburetors and dual exhausts with a four-speed manual transmission. At first, it was presented to the Pontiac board by the conspirators, with smaller engine specifications and more conservative specifications overall.

Word was carefully leaked out to dealers across the US before the Pontiac board could come to a decision, and the orders for the new option package poured in, producing a Pontiac first-model-year sales record of 32,000 cars. This was the most for any first-year Pontiac model to that time—and the second year sales outdid that!

One reason for the Tempest GTO's popularity was its design. *At left:* A 1964 Tempest LeMans GTO convertible. Its sleek simplicity complemented its performance equipment.

No automobile of the 1960s was more popular than the Ford Mustang. Small, and styled like a classic sports sedan, it had an options list that let buyers custom-tailor the car to their tastes.
    Below: A 1966 Ford Mustang coupe. The base engine was a 200-ci six cylinder. Options ran up to a 271-hp version of Ford's 289-ci (4.7-L) V-8. *Opposite:* A 1965 Mustang convertible. Note the '289 V-8' engine-designation badge on its leading fender edge.

The Pontiac GTO was variously known throughout the 1960s as 'the Goat,' 'the Judge' and a host of other monickers. With its first-year rating of 348 hp, its clean looks and slick advertising campaign, the Pontiac GTO made the wild American phenomena of the Detroit muscle car a part of the popular consciousness. With such options as the GTO's factory-installed Hurst racing shifter, it was an extremely classy offering.

Despite the GTO's great success, there was no car in the 1960s that was quite as popular as the Mustang. Ford President Lee Iacocca heeded customers who pled for a small car similar to the 1955 Thunderbird, which had since become noticeably larger.

From this seed sprang Iacocca's notion of a small, quick, easily-produced and low-priced car—something sporty but simple. Ford designers David Ash, Joe Oros and Gayle Halderman gave him what he wanted—a throwback to the speedsters of the 1920s and 1930s, with a long hood and driver and passengers tucked into a tiny cockpit. There was almost no room for luggage, but as it turned out, the public didn't mind that at all.

In the days of the flathead V-8, Ford had reigned supreme, and now it was time for another Ford epoch! This was to be the era of the 'pony car,' a Mustang-honoring name for the Mustang and the host of smaller muscle cars that emulated it.

Luxury muscle cars were also known as 'personal luxury cars,' or 'image cars.' *Below:* A 1964 Ford Thunderbird two-door landau coupe. A 300-hp, 390-ci (6.4 L) V-8 was its motive power. The interior was plush, the ride superb and the standard equipment luxurious.

Buick introduced the beautiful Riviera in 1963. With rakish good looks and a 401-ci (6.5-L) V-8 under its hood, it offered power, luxury and exemplary style. *Opposite:* A 1965 Buick Riviera. This was the last year that Buick used the original Riviera body style. As opposed to the original, however, the 1965 model featured revamped taillights, and stacked hideaway headlights that were concealed by the grilles on the leading edges of its fenders.

As first introduced to the market on 17 April 1964 (it was termed a '1964 and one-half model'), the Mustang was powered by a 170-ci (2.7 L) Ford Falcon six, plus optional engines including a larger six, a 260-ci (4.3 L) V-8, a 220-hp, 289-ci (4.7 L) V-8 or a high-performance version of same with 271 hp (which came part and parcel with a four-speed close-ratio transmission).

The first Mustangs were offered in three basic styles, including hardtop, convertible or fastback coupe, and its first nine months of production saw an incredible 680,000 cars sold.

The V-8 option was the beginning of a performance progression that was right in line with Ford's famous 'Total Performance' policy. The Mustang was a fad in itself! An astonishingly long list of options allowed the Mustang buyer to design a machine that ranged from spartan minimalism to opulent excess in trim, interior, instrumentation, power plant, handling package and other aspects of the vehicle.

Speaking of legends, the 1963 Ford Thunderbird had, as a standard engine, a 330-hp 390 (6.4 L) V-8, while a 390 V-8 of 340 hp, with three Holley two-barrel carburetors, was also available.

The 'T-bird's' styling was changed in 1964. The car now had highly sculptured sides, a longer hood, a shorter roof line, a larger hood scoop and headlights mounted at the fender edge—as opposed to the inboard-mounted lights of the 1963 models. Also, the new taillights were lateral, rectangular bars.

Among these luxury muscle cars, however, the stylish, fast and powerful Buick Riviera was the sensation of 1963. While this and other Buick performance cars weighed more than the typical muscle car of the era, it was an attempt on the part of Buick to garner, if not the youth market per se, then at least the market of the 'young at heart.'

At the time, the Buick Riviera seemed a slightly more conservative, and definitely heavier, fastback companion to the Corvette. Given what had now become traditional Buick heaviness, the Riviera still had considerable power and speed, with a 325-hp 401-ci (6.6 L) engine.

The base price of the first-year Riviera was $4333 from the factory. Its large V-8 was mated to a Turbine Drive automatic transmission. An extensive list of Riviera standard equipment included power steering; power brakes; two-speed windshield wipers with washers; backup lights; a glare-proof rearview mirror; a parking brake signal light; a safety buzzer; Riviera wheel covers; an electric clock; a license plate frame; a padded instrument panel; a trip mileage odometer; front and rear bucket seats; an interior smoking set; a deep-pile carpet; courtesy lights; foam-padded seat cushions; a center console; frameless side windows; and a heater/defroster unit.

Riviera options included air conditioning; Electro-Cruise; cornering lights; power door locks; a power trunk release; seat belts; a Sonomatic radio; a Wonderbar radio; a rear seat speaker; Soft-Ray glass; a rear window defroster; chrome door guards; a remote-control sideview mirror; power windows; a Guide-Matic dimmer; a Twilight Sentinel; a fuel filler lock; a litter basket; a tissue dispenser; seat covers; a spotlight; carpet covers; carpet savers; and a deluxe trunk mat.

While this was all impressive, the future would bring car owners the ability to choose the music they would hear on their car sound systems, and the sound itself would improve dramatically as well. Even stereo—*the* by-word for audio buffs in the new decade—would become *de rigueur*, and eventually, *passé.*

A STYLE ESTABLISHED

Below and opposite: Views of a 1966 Pontiac Tempest GTO convertible. The GTO was now officially a distinct line, much as was the Tempest LeMans from which it had developed. Note its clean, flowing lines—a classic 1960s 'look.'

Like most other special Detroit models, the Corvette came with a long list of options, but in its case, the options were predominately engineering parts—gear ratios, suspension packages and engine parts. This served to keep the Corvette on track as a competitive sports car, although it was larger than many. Corvettes also saw plenty of action at the drag strip and in road racing. It was a bit encumbered at the drag strip by its independent suspension, but did passably well in sports car events, and was a sure attention-getter, with a prestige all its own, on the street. All in all, the Corvettes of the mid-1960s continued to build a legend.

Unfortunately for them, the 427 (6.9 L) Cobras were now a reality. However, these cars were essentially hand-built, and could not be produced in sufficient quantity to meet FIA approval for road racing in the 1965 season—but then again, Ferrari ran into the same problem. So, the Cobras won the 1965 FIA GT championship with 1964 equipment.

The following year, the 427 (6.9 L) Cobras were allowed to compete in a new classification under FIA rules. This newly-created category also included the competition-only Ford GT 40 coupes, a fact that dampened Ford Motor Company's sponsorship of the Shelby competition Cobras. Shelby therefore withdrew the Cobra from FIA competition. (Withdrawal of the Cobras was ameliorated for Shelby, however, in that he was given charge of Ford's GT 40 program, and produced 1-2-3 victories at Le Mans in 1966, continuing the streak in 1967–69.)

This left the Shelby Cobra racing effort without a factory sponsor, and essentially in the hands of club racers. That was just as well. Cobras dominated in the SCCA's A Production class, winning the championship from 1965–68, inclusive, and again in 1973.

As for Pontiac's bright muscle car hopes, the 'GTO' designation was catchy and was derived from a tradition of European-style road-racing cars—which prompted Pontiac to offer a ride package with the performance package. Engines got bigger, transmission ratios improved and optional rear axles were available. Over the years, there evolved a definite GTO 'look,' with a hood scoop and a wide, well-balanced and clean profile.

When Ferrari took exception to Pontiac's use of *Grand Turismo Olmogato*—GTO—Pontiac arranged a test between the two automaker's cars. En route to the test, the

The Wizard of "Aahs"...
new 1966 Fairlane convertible

FORD

Above: **Advertising for a 1966 Ford Fairlane GT convertible. Compare the lines of this car with those of the GTO on pages 64–65.**

The base engine for this car was a 335-hp, 390-ci (6.4-L) V-8, but for drag racing, there was a choice of several 427-ci (6.9-L) V-8s.

Pontiac GTO blew a piston, and a huge Pontiac Catalina stood in for it. The Catalina out-drag raced the Ferrari, but was understandably much less agile!

The GTO's three two-barrel carburetor setup operated in the following way: for cruising, only the central two-barrel was in operation. At very high rpms, or when the accelerator was trodden suddenly, the additional carburetors opened up. It was an apparatus straight from the drag racing circuit, and with an optional radical camshaft (and, eventually, Ram Air forced induction), the Pontiac was a 'factory hot rodder's' dream.

However, the Ford Mustang was *the* success story of the decade, and General Motors and Chrysler suddenly had to play catch-up, but could never quite equal the tremendous cross-cultural appeal of the sporty, friendly and low-priced little Ford product.

The Mustang had an amazing range of options, including three- or four-speed floor-shift manual transmission; a handling package; power steering; air conditioning; bench or bucket seats; and engine power options— basically, the customer could name his desire and get it with the Mustang.

However, for the utmost in Mustang performance, Ford offered cars that Carroll Shelby, of Ford AC Cobra fame, had stamped with his signature super-wide racing stripes. These were essentially Cobras with Mustang bodies.

In 1965, Ford's Thunderbolt Fairlanes had a tough time in A/Stock, as they were up against Dodges and Plymouths equipped with Chrysler Corporation's tremendously powerful 'hemi' V-8s. In 1966, however, Ford came up with an answer to the Chrysler Corporation hemis.

This answer was, in fact, Ford's favorite drag racing project: a single-overhead-cam hemispherical combustion chamber 427 (6.9 L) V-8, a test bed engine that could produce over 600 hp with carburetion, and was first shoe-horned into Mustang and Falcon bodies, for competition in the Factory Experimental class. Fiberglass Mercury Comet Cyclones equipped with the Ford hemi made the names of 'Dyno Don' Nicholson and Bill Shrewsbury much feared indeed. These were called 'Comet Boss Dragsters.' They did wheelstands at will and blew the doors off the competition.

Needless to say, the Thunderbolt Fairlanes also inherited the very-quickly-legendary Ford 'hemi' (or 'cammer' as it was alternately called), and the Thunderbolts were

back in action. Ford 'hemis' also appeared in all-out dragsters, aka 'rails,' which were essentially superlight, super-strong frames with minimal cockpits, in-and-out boxes instead of transmissions and fuel-injected, supercharged, ultra-high compression engines producing over 1000 hp. Some of these 'rails' run on gasoline, but the ultimate rails run on such heady combinations as nitrotoluene and alcohol, and are affectionately called 'fuelers.'

Famed drag racers such as Don Prudhomme and Connie Kalitta campaigned Ford hemi rails with great success. Also, in 1966, the first of the true 'funny cars' appeared. These were essentially rails with fiberglass-replica Mercury Comet bodies covering them. Thus began a fad that would eventually involve models from every major American manufacturer.

The Ford hemi was as yet too potent to be offered as a street option, and was thus not qualifiable as a NASCAR stock car engine.

Therefore, Chrysler Corporation's hemi dominated NASCAR ovals, as they (at least in part) 'owned' the dragstrip. Dodge hemis found their way to the street in 1965, as optional equipment for the larger Dodges and Plymouths, such as the Coronet, Custom 880, Polara, Monaco and Belvedere Satellite.

The optional four-speed standard transmission was the way to go with these 'street hemis.' The standard Chrysler Corporation warranties did not apply for these 'bruisers,' however. That same year saw factory-sponsored altered-wheelbase Dodge and Plymouth drag-racing-prepared cars entering the Factory Experimental Class and doing battle with Ford and Mercury SOHCs and Chevrolet 'porcupines.'

When Ford brought out the Mustang, Plymouth acted swiftly, and hastily reworking the compact Valiant design by adding a fastback, they brought out the 1965 Plymouth Barracuda. Initially, the first Barracuda featured either of two six-cylinder engines or a 180-hp, 273-ci (4.4 L) V-8. The Barracuda's second year saw the Formula S package, which upped the 273's output to 235 hp and gave the car a pretty good handling package.

Of course, other carmakers were not totally out of the performance picture. The Buick Skylark Gran Sport, an outstanding muscle car for that company, was introduced in 1966. It had a 401-ci (6.6 L) engine that produced 325 hp, and a 340-hp version of this V-8 was optional.

Also, like the Chevelle and the later Camaro, the diminutive 1965 Chevy II sported a series of engines that topped out with the Nova SS option, a 327-ci engine (5.4 L) of 350 hp. Chevelles, especially, saw much action at the drag strip, where the 396 (6.5 L) 'porcupine' engine and its larger ramifications waged war with the hemi Fords and Chryslers.

It was somewhat of a surprise that American Motors made an attempt on the youth market with the Rambler Marlin of 1965. This car was essentially a Rambler Classic with a fastback roof, and engine choices that included two six-cylinder engines, or two V-8s of 283 ci (4.7 L) or 327 ci (5.4 L), respectively.

In the luxury market for 1965, Cadillac offered the Calais, which replaced the Series 6200 that year. Curved side windows with frameless glass were one of several new touches for all Cadillac models.

Standard Calais equipment included power brakes; power steering; automatic transmission; dual backup lights; windshield washers; dual speed wipers; a remote-controlled outside rear view mirror; a visor vanity mirror;

and front and rear safety belts. The options offered for all Cadillac lines were, as usual, enough to make the cars veritable rolling galleries of convenience and comfort items.

The standard engine was a cast-iron 429-ci (seven L) V-8 of 340 hp. For all models but the Fleetwood series, a new perimeter frame design allowed the mounting of the engine six inches forward of the position it occupied in earlier designs: therefore, the interior transmission hump could be substantially reduced, allowing more leg room for front-seat passengers.

The 1965 Cadillac DeVille was available as a coupe, two sedans and a convertible model, each variously designated as Coupe DeVille, Sedan DeVille or Convertible DeVille.

The Eldorado had that year become a one-model designation under the Fleetwood umbrella. It was now strictly a convertible, with standard equipment like that found on the lower models, plus six-way power seats (for cars with bench seating); power vent windows; a glare-proof rear-view mirror; automatic level control; and an improved

Below: A 1966 Chevrolet Chevelle Super Sport coupe. This car was equipped with a 396-ci (6.5-L) V-8 version of the famed Chevrolet 'mystery' engine.

Note, too, the clean lines that had come to typify the 1960s muscle car. It was, in a sense, an 'incognito' look, though it was quite eye-pleasing.

Below: A 1966 Chevrolet convertible. A wide choice of engines included 396-ci (6.5-L) and 427-ci (6.9-L) V-8s, and standard shift transmissions were mandatory with these large engines.

Below opposite: A 1966 Rambler Marlin. This car was basically a Rambler Classic with a fastback roof and a few other cosmetic touches. The power plant in this car was a 270-hp 327-ci (5.4-L).

Above opposite: An advertisement for Rambler's 1965 Classic models.

Turbo-Hydramatic transmission. The Fleetwood Sixty-Special subseries had the same standard features as the Eldorado, excepting the six-way power seats.

The Cadillac Fleetwoods stylistically adhered more closely to the lines of earlier years than their contemporaries. This is a peculiarity of really prestigious cars: they can't afford to depart too swiftly from a tradition, as the wealthy, successful customers who buy them tend to distrust untested extravagance.

The 1965 Fleetwood 75 Series offered a nine-passenger sedan and a nine-passenger limousine. They came with all power controls found in the Eldorado, and added map and courtesy lights to the standard equipment list. There was, however, no standard level control—too suddenly innovative. The limousine for that year cost $5260. It should be noted that Cadillac also did a reasonably good yearly business through the selling of commercial chassis—for ambulances, hearses and such.

As of 1965, the Lincoln Continental had changed very little from its early-1960s, squared-off configuration. Standard equipment on every 1965 Continental included a 320-hp, 430-ci (seven L) V-8; an automatic transmission; power steering; dual exhausts; a visor vanity mirror; a trip odometer; a transistorized radio with rear speaker; undercoating; a walnut appliqué or padded dashboard; a heater and defroster unit; six-way power seats; a power radio antenna; a remote-control outside rearview mirror; power brakes; carpeting; windshield washers; and power door locks.

Continental types offered in 1965 were a four-door sedan, a four-door convertible and an executive limousine. Optional equipment included a directed power differential; air conditioner/heater unit; individually adjustable front seats; a power trunk lock; an automatic headlight dimmer; an emergency flasher; an AM/FM push-button radio; speed control; an adjustable steering wheel; special

leather trim (standard in the convertible model); tinted glass; door-edge guards; and a closed crankcase emission reduction system.

As for Chrysler Corporation's luxury cars, the Custom Imperial series had been dropped after 1963, and for 1965, an otherwise full Imperial line was offered.

The LeBaron Imperial's offerings consisted solely of a six-person, four-door hardtop. The LeBaron differed from the Crown Imperial in having a more luxurious interior, with six-way power bench seats.

The Crown Imperial series had, as standard equipment, power brakes; power windows; power steering; carpeting; an electric clock; a padded dashboard; and a remote-control sideview mirror. Two- and four-door hardtops and a two-door convertible were offered. The engine was the 413-ci (6.8 L) V-8 used previously, upgraded to 340 hp, and was mated to the Torqueflite automatic transmission to provide motive power for the entire Imperial line.

This was the last year that the custom-built Crown Imperial was offered. Strictly an eight-person, four-door limousine with a choice of six-window styling or blind rear roof quarter panels, it was as fabulous a car as the earlier versions had been. The factory price for this car was $16,000.

Optional Imperial equipment for 1965 included air conditioning; speed-level control; an automatic headlight dimmer; a rear window defogger; door guards; electric door locks; headrests; a sideview mirror; two-tone paint; six-way power seats; a crankcase ventilation system; a remote-control trunk lock; an AM Touch-tuner radio with power antenna and rear speaker; an AM/FM radio with power antenna and rear speaker; a rear reverberator speaker; retractable seat belts; an adjustable steering wheel; a Sure-Grip differential; tinted glass; whitewall tires; leather trim; individual front seat trim; and a vinyl roof.

In the less-expensive full-size realm, the 1965 Buick

Five powerful reasons for the new excitement in the Rambler Classic

Below: A 1966 Imperial Crown series four-door hardtop. The name confusion between the low-level Crown series and the high-level Crown Imperial (see the caption on page 24) would prevail no more. In 1965, the ultra-expensive Ghia-built Crown Imperial was dropped from the Imperial roster.

Even so, the Crown series cars were very refined, and the upper-level LeBaron series sustained Imperial's prestige among American luxury cars.

Opposite: A 1965 Cadillac DeVille convertible. In Cadillac tradition, the name is more properly given as 'Convertible DeVille.' This was the only convertible that Cadillac offered, and it was surely posh enough for any fresh-air aficionado.

Electra underwent a styling change that produced a car that gave even more of an impression of heaviness than its forebears, with deeper sides, and a general squaring-off of contours—even the four ventiports were presented as rectangles.

The engine and transmission was a 325-hp, 401-ci (6.6 L) V-8 attached to a Super Turbine automatic transmission. The Electra Custom had taken the place of the 225 this year, and the types offered were as follows: a four-door sedan, a four-door hardtop, a two-door sport coupe and a convertible—all with six-passenger capacity.

General Motors' perennial favorite, Chevrolet, had made a philosophy of building cars that were just a touch classier-looking than Fords, but had never really brought out an attempt at luxury. That changed with the introduction of the Caprice sport sedan option on the Impala line in 1965. This option proved so successful that Caprice became its own line in 1966, offering a two-door coupe, a four-door hardtop and two station wagon variants.

Plush cloth or vinyl interiors; simulated wood interior accents; exterior pinstriping; and woodgrain side molding

on station wagons were some of the features of the new Caprice models. With a 213.2-inch overall length, and a stock 283-ci (4.7 L) V-8—with optional engines of up to 427 ci (6.9 L)—and a full option list including air conditioning; tinted glass; power steering; power brakes; an AM/FM radio; and a vinyl roof, the Caprice was a car that could fulfill your fantasies of owning a prestige car.

The factory price for a four-door hardtop was $3063, and you could pile on the options so that, for under $5000, you could have a car that 'did everything but brush your teeth for you.'

Meanwhile, such lower-price Chevrolet lines as Biscayne and Bel Air featured sedan and station wagon models for the car owner who was looking for economy and enough room to haul a growing family. These lower-price lines were extremely popular, and, as well as offering utility, had the basic styling of the higher-level lines, and offered the illusion of sportiness.

Chrysler New Yorkers for 1965 were offered as two four-door sedans, two four-door station wagons, a two-door coupe and a two-door convertible. By comparison, the

lower-price Newport line offered three sedans, two station wagons, one coupe and one convertible model.

The New Yorker power train included a 340-hp, 413-ci (6.8 L) V-8, mated to an automatic transmission. Standard equipment—some of which was offered on the Newport line—included power steering; power brakes; foam-cushion seats; an electric clock; a deluxe steering wheel; windshield washers; a padded dashboard; a remote-control sideview mirror; backup lights; parking brake lights; map lights; stone shields; and sill moldings.

Optional equipment included a 360-hp, 413-ci (6.8 L) V-8 for the 300L (1964 had seen the last really high-performance offering in the ram-induction 390-hp, 413-ci (6.8 L) engine for the 300K); a close-ratio four-speed manual shift transmission; a positive-traction rear axle; a choice of rear axle gear ratios; power windows; six-way power seats; power door locks; a heater and defroster unit; air conditioning; a Golden Tone radio; an AM/FM radio; a Golden Touch tuner; a rear seat speaker; seat

belts; a handling package including heavy-duty springs, shocks, sway bar and brakes; an adjustable steering wheel; undercoating; tinted glass; a day/night mirror; and a remote-control sideview mirror.

A basic 1965 New Yorker four-door hardtop sedan came with a factory price of $4336, while a 300L two-door hardtop coupe sold for $4251, reflecting the fact that the Series 300 was even then descending from the heights it had once occupied. On the other hand, the 1965 Newport four-door hardtop sedan bore a factory price of $3582.

Dodge began its move toward the lower-priced luxury market with the Monaco, which was essentially a higher-trim Polara. It was a luxury two-door hardtop, developed in 1965 to compete with Pontiac's Gran Prix. Standard equipment included foam-cushion front seats; front seat belts; chrome windshield and rear window moldings; and deluxe hubcaps with recessed central 'spinner.'

The Monaco was expanded to a full line, still sharing Polara styling, in 1966, and offered sedans, hardtops, station wagons and a new, even more luxurious model, the Monaco 500.

Engine options ranged up to the 426-ci (6.9 L) 'hemi' V-8 and the 440-ci (7.2 L) conventional V-8 that I have discussed in the portion of this text that deals with muscle cars. The base level engine for the 1966 Monaco 500 was a 325-hp, 383-ci (6.3 L) V-8, backed by a three-speed Torqueflite automatic transmission or an optional four-speed, floor-shift standard transmission. Options on the Monoco 500 included air conditioning; power brakes; power steering; power door locks; power seats; an AM/FM radio with rear reverb speaker; an electric clock; and a rear window defogger.

The intermediate Coronet line carried four sedans and a station wagon, while the full-size Polara line offered one sedan, one convertible, two hardtops and two station wagons. The Coronet and the Polara lines had at that point been the bearers of much of Dodge's performance equipment, as well as doing duty as excellent family cars in less aggressive formats.

Ford produced its own version of the lower-level luxury car in the Galaxie 500 LTD, which was essentially a high-level trim option on the full-size Galaxie in 1965. The factory price for a 1966 Galaxie 500 LTD hardtop sedan was $3278—which meant that an owner could pile the options on if that was desired, or could leave it relatively plain, and

Doubling up on their model designations was a favorite vice of Chrysler Corporation. As with the Imperial Crown series/Crown Imperial cars, Chrysler maintained the legendary Chrysler 300 cars through 1965, but introduced a low-level line of cars also designated '300' in 1962.

The difference between the designations was that the 300s that had once dominated motorsports in America were given a letter suffix that coincided with the model year of the car—thus, the 1960 300 was the 300F, while the 1965 version was the 300L (they skipped the letter 'I' for aesthetic reasons). After the 300L was produced in 1965, the letter-series 300s were dicontinued and only the lower-level 300 remained. *Below left:* A lower-level 1965 Chrysler 300 two-door hardtop coupe.

Above left: A 1966 Chrysler 300 hardtop coupe. If it was not quite the plush, powerful car the letter-series 300 had been, it was still not a disgrace to the '300' designation, as its base-level engine was a 325-hp, 383-ci (6.3-L) V-8, and its appointments were suitably plush.

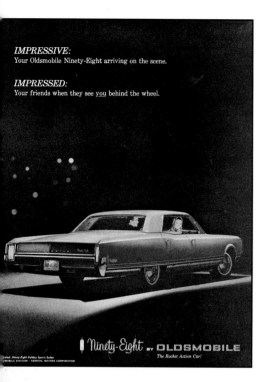

Oldsmobile offered drivers a selection of cars for performance and plushness. At the top of the line in the 1960s was the Ninety-Eight series.

Above: An advertisement for a mid-1960s Ninety-Eight Holiday hardtop sedan. As can be seen here, Oldsmobile had achieved a harmonious blend of curves and simplicity in their mid-decade designs.

Opposite: A 1965 Oldsmobile F-85 Cutlass convertible. Offered in coupe versions as well, the F-85 Cutlass was the recipient of Oldsmobile's answer to the Pontiac GTO — the optional 4-4-2 power and handling package.

The 400-ci (6.5-L) V-8 with four-barrel carburetor and dual exhaust pipes that was part of the 4-4-2 package had an output of 345 hp.

still have a car that appeared rather distinguished in a low-price kind of way.

For the year 1965, Oldsmobile styling continued to pleasingly combine the overall look of the Lincoln Continental and the Pontiac LeMans, with slightly more formal touches given the large-wheelbase Ninety-Eight. The Starfire had been with the Ninety-Eight at the top of the Oldsmobile range for two years.

The Starfire was originally offered in 1961, but this glimpse of its next-to-last year in production may serve to give a general idea of the level of luxury provided by this car.

Starfires were offered as two types: a two-door coupe and a convertible. The power plant for these full-size cars was a 370-hp, 425-ci (6.9 L) V-8. Standard equipment included: T-stick controlled Turbo-Hydramatic transmission; power steering; power brakes; bucket seats; courtesy lamps; a center console; a tachometer; a padded dash; a parking brake signal lamp; a deluxe steering wheel; special wheel covers; windshield washers; power windows; power seats; and a choice of vinyl, leather or cloth upholstery.

The Ninety-Eights, on the other hand, had a 360-hp, 425-ci (6.9 L) V-8 connected to a Turbo-Hydramatic transmission. There were five types offered in 1965: Town Sedan; Holiday Sedan; and Luxury Sedan, all four-door cars; Sports Coupe; and convertible, both two-door cars. Standard equipment included power steering; power brakes; power windows; a clock; a padded dash; foam padded seats; a parking brake signal lamp; a deluxe steering wheel; special wheel covers; two-speed windshield wipers and washers; courtesy lights; a glove compartment light; front seat belts; and a choice of leather, vinyl or cloth upholstery.

Optional equipment included air conditioning; a side-view mirror; an AM/FM radio; a power antenna; a rear speaker; Cruise Control; tilt-wheel steering; and a rear window defogger.

The Starfire was not offered after the 1966 year, which saw the introduction of a very surprising luxury offering: the front-wheel-drive Toronado. There is more about this interesting car in a later discussion of luxury muscle cars.

Oldsmobile's lower-level full-size lines for 1966 had good market staying power. The ever-popular Vista Cruiser station wagon was offered in two levels of six- and

nine-passenger versions each; and the Delta Eighty-Eight was offered in coupe, convertible and sedan variants.

Oldsmobile styling in the mid-1960s was unique, with its full wheel well cutouts and flowing fender lines. There was an attractive harmony of design that gave each car a distinguished appearance.

Lower-price full-size Fords included the Custom and the Galaxie, both of which had higher-trim '500' levels; and the Ranch Wagon, Country Sedan and Country Squire station wagons. As with Chevrolet, Chrysler and Dodge, these lower-level lines could be equipped with options to answer to a number of requirements.

Standard LTD trim was chrome windshield and rear window moldings; nylon carpeting; arm rests with ashtrays on all doors; two sun visors; a chrome horn ring; a chrome hood ornament; stamped aluminum rocker panel moldings; two-tone vinyl trim on the inside of the doors and seats; simulated walnut instrument panel and door accents; deep-cushion seats; a gabardine headliner and

sun visors; a full complement of courtesy lights; a full instrument panel lighting group; and a lighted glove compartment and ashtrays.

This second-year LTD was offered as either a four-door hardtop or a two-door fastback coupe, and a wealth of options were available to make it even more of an invocation of the spirit of luxury.

A squared-off body styling treatment for 1965 made the Mercury Park Lane resemble the Lincoln somewhat. A padded dash; padded visors; a full complement of courtesy lights; a visor-mounted mirror; and a trip odometer, plus a luxurious interior in general and a strip of chrome trim just above the rocker panels were standard features of this 218.4-inches-long car.

The Park Lane's base engine was a 300-hp, 390-ci (6.4 L) V-8, coupled to an automatic transmission. Air conditioning; power steering; power brakes; power windows; bucket seats with a reclining passenger side seat; an AM/FM radio; a sports package in two-door hardtop and convertible versions; custom wheel covers; and a vinyl roof were among the Park Lane options.

The Park Lane was offered in four-door Breezeway sedan, four- and two-door hardtop and convertible models. The sedan featured a Mercury exclusive that had been popular in the Monterey for years. This was a rear window that could be cranked (or powered) down, to provide the 'breezeway' that gave the Park Lane sedan its name. The base factory price for a Park Lane Breezeway sedan was $3301 in 1965.

In 1965, the Pontiac Grand Prix moved into its own after having been offered for two years as a variant. Still a two-door hardtop coupe, it had a very bold grille treatment that featured large 'air slots' separated by widely-spaced vertical bars, and incorporated the front turn signals in floating boxes at its extremities.

Fender skirts were also a feature, as was the 'Coke-bottle' body shape that was a Pontiac hallmark that year. Standard equipment included front and rear arm rests;

courtesy lights; padded armrests; monotone naugahyde upholstery; and a choice of bench or buckets seats with console and console-mounted tachometer. The base engine was a 389-ci (6.4 L) V-8 with 325–333 hp, depending on transmission used.

Options were even more abundant this year than in previous years, and included—in addition to those cited for 1964—remote-control rearview mirror, Super-Lift shock absorbers, remote-control trunk lid and more. The Catalina and Star Chief continued to uphold the bottom of the Pontiac full-size line, and were fairly popular family cars, offering a sense of safety through a reassuring bulkiness, with a sense of good styling.

The Plymouth Sport Fury of 1965 was one of two top-level offerings for Plymouth that year. The other was the Fury III (two steps up from the Fury I, and one step up from the not-so-plain Fury II). The Fury III was offered in four-door sedan and hardtop, two-door hardtop and convertible and four-door six- and nine-passenger station wagon models.

'65 Pontiac Grand Prix.
Now the only question is: who has the year's second-best-looking car?

At left: A 1966 Pontiac Bonneville two-door hardtop. Note the so-called 'Coke bottle' shape that was then Pontiac's hallmark full-size design.

The top engine option for this car was a 376-hp, 421-ci (6.8-L) V-8 with three two-barrel carburetors, but its place as the hottest Pontiac had been usurped by the Tempest GTO.

Above: Advertising art for the 1965 Pontiac Grand Prix. Note the text of this promotion, which emphasizes the attractiveness of Pontiac body styling.

The Sport Fury, on the other hand, was offered as either a two-door hardtop or convertible. Body styling for full-size Plymouths featured vertical quad headlights, clean, forward-thrusting lines and formal sedan or cantilever roof treatments for sedans and hardtops, respectively.

Standard Fury III equipment included seat belts; foam seats; carpets; courtesy lights; and backup lamps. The Sport Fury had all that plus special wheel covers; bucket seats; a central console; a deluxe steering wheel; and rear fender skirts. The standard engine was a 230-hp, 318-ci (5.2 L) V-8.

Options included a Torqueflite automatic transmission; a four-speed standard transmission with floor shift; engines up to a 415-hp, 426-ci (6.9 L) V-8 (the 'hemi' was not available on Furies); a positraction differential; power steering; air conditioning; a rear window defogger; a padded dashboard; tinted glass; power windows; power seats; an AM/FM radio; a tachometer; an adjustable steering wheel; and other convenience items. The factory base price for a 1965 Sport Fury convertible was $3164, as compared to $3006 for a Fury III convertible.

The year 1966 saw the rise of the Fury VIP—yet another high-level Plymouth line—which supplanted the Fury III, making that line now a high-trim level, but not the cream of the crop. Sport Furies had many of the same features as the year before. The Fury VIP was offered originally as a four-door hardtop, and then, halfway through the model year, two-door hardtops were added to the line.

The Fury VIP was a more conservative car that balanced out the sportiness of the Sport Fury. It had the Fury III standard features (similar to those found on 1965 models), and instead of adding on bucket seats and console à la the Sport Fury, the Fury VIP added on special side moldings with wood grain inserts, fender skirts, center arm rest seats and reading lamps mounted on window pillars. A full list of options was available.

The Belvedere was the Plymouth mid-size line, offering three levels—Belvedere I and II, and Belvedere Satellite. Many of the options listed above were available on the Belvederes, and the Satellite was the 'hot' offering. It was, in fact, the 1966 Plymouth most likely to contain the 'street hemi' under its hood, and roared the length of many a drag strip in winning time.

For the record, Belvederes were offered in sedan, hardtop coupe and station wagon models, and were an

Let yourself Go Plymouth '66

These pages: Promotional artwork and a slogan for the 1966 Plymouth Fury line. The two-door model is a Sport Fury hardtop coupe, and the four-door is a Fury VIP hardtop sedan.

At the top of the options list for both of these high-level Plymouths was a 365-hp, 440-ci (6.5-L) V-8.

By contrast, the contemporaneous Plymouth Belvedere Satellite—an intermediate-size Plymouth—was granted the famed 426-ci (6.9-L) hemi engine option, with 425 hp.

extremely popular family, business and police car. There was a pleasant conciseness in their blunt good looks, and the cantilever treatment given to the hardtop sedans made them a premium item among those who sought a car with a 'touch of dash.'

The Rambler Ambassador continued as that company's top line, with the Classic serving in sporty mid-line duty. Studebaker brought out a revived version of its old Commander line, and added a new line, the Cruiser, for 1965; but 1966 would be the last model year that Studebakers were offered.

Meanwhile, the taught, clean lines of the 1963–64 Buick Riviera were improved upon in the 1965 Riviera, by the subtle but effective step of filling in the false louvers in front of the car's rear wheel.

Also, the 1965 Riviera acquired a 425-ci (6.9 L)

Buick's 360-hp, 425-ci (6.9-L) 'Super Wildcat V-8' found its way under the hood of Buick's stylish luxury muscle car, the Riviera, as well as the more conventional Skylark. This was made possible by the Gran Sport option.

Opposite: A promotional photo of a 1966 Buick Riviera. Note the styling differences between this and the 1965 Riviera just discussed.

Above right: A 1966 Buick Skylark Gran Sport hardtop.

V-8 engine of 340 hp—a 'Super Wildcat' 425 (6.9 L), with two four-barrel carburetors, producing 360 hp, was optionally available, and included large-diameter dual exhausts; a positraction differential; and bright-metal engine accent treatment. This package was known as the Gran Sport option.

This year, the Riviera also sported stacked quad headlights that were hidden by roll-away grilles on the leading fender edges. The taillights were melded into the bumper bar. Standard equipment included a Super Turbine transmission; power steering; power brakes; backup lights; two-speed window wipers with washers; a safety buzzer; a map light; an adjustable-tilt steering wheel; an automatic trunk light; license plate frames; instrument panel safety pads; full carpeting; double door release handles; walnut paneling on the instrument panel; front bucket seats; an electric clock; and a non-glare rearview mirror.

Optional equipment included custom interiors with carpeted lower doors; air conditioning; four- or six-way power seats; an AM or AM/FM radio; a remote-control sideview mirror; tinted glass; a four-note horn; a tachometer; an automatic trunk release; Electro-Cruise; and cornering lights.

A sleek new look came to grace the Riviera in 1966, with an unbroken frontal plane made possible by a unique 'hideaway' headlight treatment. The car's lines were soft-

Oldsmobile reopened the case for front-wheel drive when the company brought out the Toronado in 1966.

Above and opposite: Examples of the sleek, 1966 Oldsmobile Toronado, showing the smooth silhouette that made Toronado styling so distinctive. Two levels of trim were offered—standard and deluxe.

With a first-year standard V-8 of 385 hp, the Toronado was designed to make an impression when the driver trod the accelerator. Front-wheel drive also meant no driveshaft hump, so there was plenty of leg-room for Toronado passengers.

ened, and a subtlety of line that hadn't been seen for years in a Buick was the result.

The Gran Sport option this year consisted of chrome cosmetic treatment for the standard engine; a positraction differential; heavy-duty shock absorbers; and special tires. It did not include the Super Wildcat 425 (6.9 L) that year, so Riviera owners had to content themselves with the standard 340-hp 425 (6.9 L) V-8.

Standard equipment included much that was offered on previous Rivieras, plus all-around seat belts and a new instrument panel with some unique touches. The Super Turbine automatic was still the only transmission offered. Optional equipment was also similar to that offered in 1965.

Oldsmobile had a surprise for the motoring world in 1966: the front-wheel-drive fastback Toronado. This was the first practical full-size front-wheel-drive American car since the Cord of the 1930s. Featuring sporty bulges over the wheel wells, distinctive, slotted wheel design; ultra-smooth lines; and 'hideaway headlights' (a feature that would become a craze among automakers of the late 1960s), the Toronado was as distinctive in appearance as it was distinctive in its engineering.

Strictly a two-door coupe, the 1966 Toronado had, as standard equipment, a 385-hp, 425-ci (6.9 L) engine; a Turbo-Hydramatic transmission; power steering and power brakes; a Strato-bench front seat; foam seat cushions; a special chrome molding package; carpeting; an electric clock; backup lamps; deluxe armrests; courtesy lamps; a sideview mirror; a parking brake signal lamp; and a choice of vinyl, leather or cloth interior.

Optional equipment included air conditioning; tinted windows; power seats; headrests; a power trunk opener; a vinyl roof; a sports console; Cruise Control; a tilt steering column; a tachometer; a power antenna; a rear radio speaker; an AM/FM radio; power door locks; and a rear window defroster. Two ranges were offered: standard and deluxe, with base prices of $4585 and $4779.

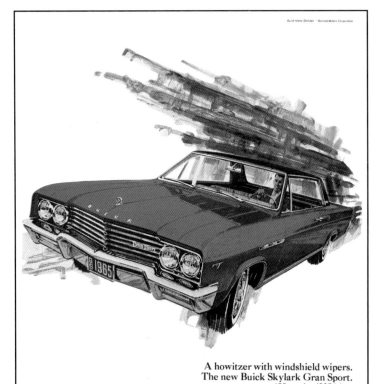

A howitzer with windshield wipers.
The new Buick Skylark Gran Sport.
400 cu. in./325 bhp.

There is mounting evidence that our engineers have turned into a bunch of performance enthusiasts.

First they stuff the Wildcat full of engine. Then the Riviera Gran Sport. And now this, the Skylark GS, which is almost like having your own, personal-type nuclear deterrent. We've just turned it loose on our dealers. (See the Buick dealers run.)

Aside from all those cubic inches and horses and 445 lb-ft of torque, just what is this thing

that our engineers have unleashed?

It's a pretty sophisticated suspension package, for one thing: Heavy-duty springs and shocks, plus a stabilizer bar that's about twice as stiff as the normal Skylark's. Axle wind-up is snubbed by heavy-duty upper control arm bushings.

It's also a floor-shift 3-speed, with all forward gears synchronized. Dual exhausts. A reinforced convertible frame to handle all that extra torque. 7.75x14 tires. All standard equipment.

Want to go the 4-speed route? There's a close-ratio unit available. Axle ratios? They read like this—2.78, 3.08, 3.23, 3.36, 3.55, and 3.73:1. Well, there's some of the evidence. Performance enthusiasts, that's what they are. More power to them.

The Buick Skylark
Gran Sport

Above: That Buick was serious about its bid for the performance market is evidenced by this advertisement for the 1965 Skylark Gran Sport. 'A howitzer with windshield wipers,' indeed....

At right: A promotional photo of a 1966 Buick Wildcat, a full-size car that the company often touted for its performance. The spoked wheels shown here were standard, as was a 325-hp, 401-ci (6.6-L) V-8. A 340-hp, 425-ci (6.9-L) V-8 was optional.

The mid-1960s luxury muscle car market was very strong. For 1965, a 300-hp, 390-ci (6.4 L) engine was Ford Thunderbird standard. Three types were offered, all with two doors and all with four-passenger capacity—hardtop, landau and convertible.

Among the many standard features on the 1965 Thunderbird were disk brakes; an automatic transmission; and sequential turn signals. Optional equipment included power windows; air conditioning; tinted windows; leather seats; power seats; an AM/FM radio; a vacuum trunk release; and deluxe wheel covers.

The following year, the T-bird had the same body, but with subtle touches that gave it a new lease on freshness. The tuck-under grille was more sharply angled and featured a large Thunderbird emblem in its middle, and the rear taillights were set behind a single red plastic bar that ran the width of the car.

The standard Thunderbird bucket-seats-up-front and semi-buckets in the rear still applied, and a new power plant standard was established in a 315-hp, 390-ci (6.4 L) V-8, with a 345-hp, 428-ci (seven L) V-8 as an option. The 1966 Thunderbird hardtop coupe cost $4935 from the factory; the landau cost $4552; and the convertible $4845.

The compact car market's Rambler American was essentially the same in 1965 as it had been in 1964, but emerged in 1966 with a new, more squared-off body styling, and with a new top-line model, the Rambler Rogue, which was a two-door hardtop with a 290-ci (4.7 L) V-8 and a four-speed manual transmission. That year also saw American Motors Company beginning its transition from the Rambler nomenclature to AMC, a phenomena that was advertised in such ways as 'Come see the new Americans at your Rambler/AMC dealer.'

Meanwhile, the Studebaker Lark was fast fading into history, like its parent company. The Lark name essentially became a byline on Cruiser and Commander models in 1965, and the company closed up its automaking facilities after model year 1966.

The Ford Falcon continued to offer its base-level, station wagon and Futura lines in 1965. The 'hot' engine was the 289-ci (4.7 L) V-8. The cars were little changed from 1964, but featured slightly plainer grilles. As for the Falcon's drag-racing propensities, this text's muscle cars discussions treat that more fully.

In 1966, the Falcon acquired a long-nosed look that for some was an unwelcome departure from its former, pleasingly abbreviated, appearance. Ford obviously sought to take advantage of the Mustang's popularity with this vaguely Mustang-like styling, but the Falcon should have been allowed to develop in its own, already popular, mode. It was 184.3 inches in overall length, while the station wagons were 198.7 inches in overall length, and would wear its benighted long-nosed styling for the remainder of the decade.

The Mercury Comets for 1965 featured a dramatic, forward-looking but squared-off style that was considered by many auto buffs to be a classic. Standard for the Caliente this year was a vinyl roof, chrome wheels, two hood scoops and curb molding; plus a 200-hp, 289-ci (4.7 L) V-8. The Comet's exploits at the racetrack are more fully documented in the muscle cars discussions.

At 195.3 inches overall length for passenger car versions, this was the last year for the Comet as a compact car: 1966 saw the length increase to 203 inches for Comet passenger cars.

General Motors launched the Corvair line even further into the performance market in 1965, offering the full Monza line as well as an even more performance-oriented

Below: A late-1960s Falcon with the long-nosed, quasi-Mustang styling that first encumbered Falcons in 1966. The pleasing Falcon bluntness was gone.

Always a popular economy car, the Falcon also saw much action at the drag strip, bearing such unstreetable engines as Ford's experimental 427-ci (6.9-L) single-overhead-cam hemi V-8.

The Falcon's usage in the everyday world centered more on the standard Ford six-cylinder power plant than on exotic competition equipment.

Opposite: A 1966 Thunderbird landau coupe, doing rather unusual duty as a promotional vehicle. The standard engine for this posh luxury muscle car was a 390-ci (6.4-L) V-8, and a 428-ci (seven-L) V-8 was optional.

car, the Corsa, in sport coupe and convertible variants. Only the Greenbriar wagon, and Series 500 sedans and sport coupes were offered for the lower range.

The Corsa took over the performance edge from the Monza, offering 140- and 180-hp engines with which it could achieve 115 mph. The Corvair of 1965 was a somewhat safer car than had been the previous models, with wishbone rear suspension that vastly improved the handling and load-bearing of the car. Also, improved interior trim and a smoother, more flowing body style added attractiveness to these upgraded Corvairs.

This same year, however, the crusading consumer advocate Ralph Nader released his book *Unsafe at Any Speed*. In it, he targeted General Motors' approach to vehicle safety, citing the Corvair as the prime example for which the automaker should be held accountable for accidents suffered by General Motors products owners.

The really major flaw in the pre-1965 Corvair was its disastrous instability at highway speeds. The average Corvair had a standard curb weight of 2400 pounds, more than half of which was concentrated on the rear axles of the car, against the best hopes of the Corvair's designer, Ed Cole.

With so much of the car's weight concentrated on it, the independent rear suspension was inadequate. It was a simple swing-axle setup, with little support save the axles themselves, and *they* were too light to begin with. These rear axles would snap at speed, and the car would go into a dangerous spin, sometimes flipping over entirely. Cost-cutting has often been blamed for the Corvair's inadequacies.

The Plymouth Valiant was, with the Dodge Dart, becoming a mainstay for economy enthusiasts who also sought reliability and endurance. The slant-six engine would take all that an owner could do with it, and still would run for thousands upon thousands of road miles.

This era also saw the addition to the Chevy II line of the Nova series, including the Nova Super Sport, which was a two-door hardtop with performance options that are discussed in the portion of this text dealing with muscle cars. The upscale Nova line in general included a four-door sedan and a station wagon.

The year 1966 saw the introduction of a new Chevy II body style—a tasteful improvement, with a slightly more rakish rear window, without obliterating the original, pleasing lines of the little cars.

Enjoy the great outdoors in this great indoors: Comet Caliente

Above: An advertisement for the 1966 Mercury Comet Caliente convertible. Compare the look of this car with that of its cousin, the Falcon on page 87.

At left: A promotional photo of a 1965 Dodge Dart GT hardtop coupe. Its standard power plant was a 170-ci (2.7-L) slant-six, and a 273-ci (4.4-L) V-8 was optional. Dodge advertised the compact Dart as 'mildly wild' and 'loaded with room.'

Opposite: A better-designed and thus better-handling Corvair, the 1966 model came too late. Ralph Nader's 1965 book *Unsafe at Any Speed* had confirmed suspicions about earlier Corvairs, destroying the line's market appeal.

VINYL AND HORSEPOWER

One of the most striking-looking muscle cars of the late 1960s was the Corvette. The 1968 Corvette was the first year of the line to feature the 'Mako Shark' show-car styling, even though the cars were still officially called 'Corvette Stingrays.' It was Corvette's 15th anniversary, and a lot of changes had been made. The cars were larger, heavier and had dramatically larger engines, including the Chevrolet 396 (6.5 L) 'porcupine' engine, and would later acquire the monster 427 (6.9 L) engine.

Ironically, these Corvettes seemed like 'Johnnie-Come-Latelys' compared to the Shelby AC Cobra, whose side-pipes had become 'badges of honor' for owners of competition-tuned Cobras—capable of nearly 200 mph.

With more torque than it would ever *need*, the 427 (6.9 L) Cobra was so potent that it was ruled to have its own classification at the drag strip. Indeed, the 'day of the Cobra' was not over. Craig Breedlove took a Cobra to the Bonneville Salt Flats and set dozens of speed records with it.

With a relatively small market for the 427 (6.9 L) competition models, 30 unsold, unfinished competition cars were left to languish at the Shelby facility in Los Angeles. However, a plucky Shelby American field representative, Charles Beidler, saw these as potentially hot sellers for an unthought-of market: semi-competition street cars.

Equipped to run on the street with the competition 427 (6.9 L) engine, these Cobras were designated S/C, for 'semi-competition.' The only items that separated these from full-competition cars were mufflers, rubber suspension bushings, soft brake pads and radiator cooling fans.

The factory specification called for dual 600 cfm four-barrel carburetors, but many of the S/Cs were fed by a single 750 cfm Holley four-barrel, à la the full competition cars. In 1967, the last of the non-competition street 427 (6.9 L) engines (the ones that were actually powered by 428-ci [seven L] engines) were produced, and Shelby, considering the then-upcoming emissions and safety regulations, chose to let the Cobra project fold.

(On the other side of the Atlantic, the AC Company chose not to let an opportunity go by, and produced their own extension of the Cobra, the AC 428, a handsome Italianate two-seater that was powered by Ford's passenger-car 428 [seven L] engine.)

A new, sleeker, Corvette body design (see also pages 53–54) appeared in 1968. *Below:* A 1968 Corvette. *Opposite:* A customized 1968 Corvette. Note the '427' engine designation badges on the hood-mounted air intakes.

The year 1968 brought the Ford Mustang some truly big engines—a 335-hp 390 (6.4 L) V-8, and a 390-hp 427-ci (6.9 L) V-8. Depending upon the customer's taste in choosing options, the Mustang was a car that one could drive with the most sedate demeanor, or it was a car that could outperform most of the other cars on the road. The Mustang had an entire auto sales bracket all to itself from 1965–1967, and it sold phenomenally.

Mustangs set records everywhere. Carroll Shelby's very potent 'Cobra treatment' affected several versions, and meant uncompromising performance by way of high compression, a radical camshaft and either a single high-output Holley four-barrel carburetor (on smaller engines), or two Holley fours (on larger engines).

A Shelby-tuned 289-ci (4.7 L) engine powered the GT 350 (which had 306 hp); a Shelby-tuned 428-ci (seven L) engine of 425 hp made the Shelby Cobra 427 (6.9 L) Mustang (offered in 1967 only) a standout; and a somewhat detuned but still performance-oriented 428 (seven L) engine of 355 hp powered the GT 500, introduced in 1967. Shelby's Cobra Mustang line would be dropped by Ford in 1970, but Shelby stayed with the GT 350 and GT 500 cars until then. While management at Ford Motor Company took steps to detune some of these cars, they were still aggressive performers.

Because it hadn't yet been produced in sufficient quantity, and was not offered in a street variant, the Ford SOHC hemi was not legal for the NASCAR circuit. Not long after, however, Ford came up with a new performance design for their extant NASCAR 427 (6.9 L) engine.

This design involved a feature called 'tunnel-port heads,' which essentially allowed a greater volume of fuel, with a better air mixture, to flow into the engine's cylinders: this proved to be a big winner on the NASCAR circuit, and Ford products even overcame the fearsome and powerful hemi-powered NASCAR Dodges and Plymouths.

The SOHC hemi had been approved, finally, for NASCAR racing in 1967, but Ford Motor Company realized the adverse publicity that could come from running the SOHC as a stock car: in order to do so, the engine would have to be offered as an option to regular customers.

It was enough that Ford had backed the intensively hot AC Cobra, but the news that they were preparing to unleash a 600-plus-hp engine on the streets would probably have caused large segments of the citizenry to sur-

Sadly, the sprightly little Mustang was getting bigger as the years rolled on. On the other hand, Ford engineers took inspiration from Carroll Shelby and began designing their own renditions of the Shelby Mustangs. *Below:* A 1968 Mustang GT fastback coupe, with a 325-hp, 390-ci (6.4-L) under its hood.

Below: A 1967 Barracuda fastback coupe. The fastback was what most obviously distinguished the early Barracuda from the Valiant: the running gear was much the same, and non-fastback models were nearly identical.

The Barracuda did not acquire 'muscle car' engines like the 275-hp, 340-ci (5.6-L) V-8 until the 1968 model year.

round Dearborn, Michigan, with pitchforks and flaming torches, à la the old Frankenstein movies.

Ford decided not to risk it. Instead, the somewhat tamer solution of using tunnel-port heads (and in 1968, using the more streetable Boss 429 [seven L] hemi) was deemed to be the way to win on the NASCAR circuit.

It was officially known as featuring what Ford euphemistically called 'crescent' combustion chambers (by way of seeking a distinction from the Chrysler hemis), but was, for all intents and purposes, a hemi—but in less than full-competition tune, was not as potent as either Ford's own SOHC hemi or the fire-breathing Chrysler products.

Meanwhile, in 1967, Mercury brought out its Cougar line. Cougars were essentially elongated Mustangs with hideaway headlights. While none of the Cougars got the Shelby treatment that the Mustangs did, they were subject to many of the same performance options that the Comet Cyclones had, with engines that ranged from six-cylinders to V-8s of 302 (4.9 L), 352 (5.8 L) and 390 ci (6.4 L), plus a special option of a streetable 427-ci (6.9 L) V-8 of 390 hp.

Chrysler was going for performance as strongly as ever. Dodge's hot 'big car' street package for 1967 was the Coronet R/T, featuring a 350-hp, 440-ci (7.2 L) V-8 with dual exhausts and a Torqueflite automatic transmission.

In competition, Plymouth was dominant on the NASCAR ovals under the guiding hands of drivers like Richard Petty.

The hemi Plymouth Road Runner and hemi Satellite GTX, and the hemi Dodge Charger and hemi Dodge Dart were made available in 1968 as competition packages.

Dodge Coronets captured five wins on the Grand National stock car circuit that same year.

The year 1968 also saw the advent of the bumblebee-striped Coronet 'Super Bee,' which featured a high-output 383-ci (6.3 L) wedge engine, much like the Plymouth Road Runner, an intermediate that was introduced directly as a youth market offering that same year. The Plymouth Satellite GTX, on the other hand, featured a standard single four-barrel, 440-ci (7.2 L) engine, with the hemi as an option.

As of 1968, the Plymouth Barracuda had acquired a range of 318- (5.2 L), 340- (5.6 L) and 383-ci (6.3 L) engines, with optional performance packages that applied to the powertrain and handling.

General Motors was, of course, quite active in the performance market. In 1967, Chevrolet brought out their answer to the Mustang.

This car was known as the Camaro, and in true 'pony car' style, it had an incredibly long list of options, so that the buyer could tailor the car to his fancy. Officially, the basic engines available were a 140/155 hp straight six and two V-8s, in 327- (5.4 L) and 350-ci (5.7 L) versions.

There was, however, a third option that was rather quietly introduced—this was the brand-new high-performance small block V-8 engine, which was 302 ci (4.9 L), and seemed tailor-made (and it was) for the Trans-Am racing series. (GM's 307 [five L] V-8 was too large.)

This engine formed the heart of the famed Z28 racing package, which would represent the top of Camaro form until many years later. Then again, for those who wanted a drag-racing machine, there was the 396-ci (6.5 L) engine option, which was rated at 375 hp, and formed the heart of the SS 396 racing package. This 396 was one of the famed 'porcupine' engines.

The original Z28 was of no use to anyone but an all-out racer, although in later years, the designation was used to sell more ornate Camaros with detuned V-8s.

First introduced as 'senior compacts' in 1964, Chevelles of 1967 featured everything from six-cylinder engines to the SS option package, which included a top-of-the-line 396-ci (6.5 L) V-8 engine of 375 hp. Since this was the base engine of the 'porcupine' engine line, later Chevelles

would also feature 427- (6.9 L) and 454-ci (7.4 L) 'rat motors.'

Long the factory hot rod buff's friend, Pontiac had great success with their GTO, and, under the leadership of John De Lorean, were fast developing their own answer to the smaller, handier Mustang, king of the pony cars.

Soon enough, General Motors management talked De Lorean and associates into making their pony car a Camaro lookalike, and the Firebird was born in 1967. Cheaper than the Mercury Cougar, it was more expensive than either the Mustang or the Camaro.

The Firebird's top-of-the-line engine was a 335-hp V-8, later replaced by a 360-hp V-8. Then, following GM's dictum of 'no more than one horsepower per 10 pounds of body weight,' Pontiac fitted a soft metal tab to the carburetor of their 360-hp engine to create the 335-hp version — this tab was often removed by those who knew about it.

In 1968, there was a 400 (6.5 L) HO (High Output) Firebird, and numerous performance kits were brought out to improve the Firebird's flying capabilities.

Not to be left out, Oldsmobile presented a special edition of the 4-4-2, with a handling package and a 455-ci (7.4 L) V-8, in 1968.

The Rambler Marlin didn't really go over well, so American Motors tried again in 1968, scoring an immediate hit with the Javelin, a sporty four-seater with either a six-cylinder engine or a 343-ci (5.6 L) V-8.

The Javelin entered the Trans-Am racing series, and, with factory backing, almost beat the champion Mustang team. That was not all to be heard from AMC: halfway through 1968, the AMX, a sporty two-seater with Javelin styling, was unveiled. This peppy little car featured either a 343-ci (5.6 L) V-8 or a top-of-the-line 390-ci (6.4 L) V-8 with 315 hp.

Above: A 1968 Dodge Charger. With its optional 425-hp, 426-ci (6.9-L) hemi V-8, it also had a special handling package that was very good. *Car and Driver* magazine of December 1967 stated that the Charger did 'everything an automobile should do, and well.'

The Lincoln Continental continued with its classic 1960s styling, and like most full-size cars in the mid-to-late 1960s, offered a vinyl roof option. Vinyl seemed to be the big news, as it was offered in various forms as a covering for roofs and as materials for even the most luxurious interiors. The utmost in vinyl was naugahyde. Essentially, naugahyde was vinyl-coated fabric that emulated the look of real leather.

Vinyl was used to cover padded dashboards and door-liners; was used to form shoulder harnesses and seat-belts; and, in concert with denser plastics such as those used for light and heating controls and steering wheels, allowed automakers to produce cars with interiors of an unparalleled consistency of coloration. For those who found one-color interiors boring, there were a host of vinyl, plastic and formica-like materials that made cheap, light-weight chrome trim and simulated wood grain panels possible.

The American luxury muscle car world of 1967 witnessed a major restyling that gave the Ford Thunderbird a body that sloped from the cockpit back toward the tail, and forward toward the nose—with somewhat the effect of a Loewy Studebaker coupe of the early 1950s. This design featured full-width taillight plastic and a full-width grille with hideaway headlights (a favorite styling trope of the 1960s). This was also the first year that a four-door Thunderbird would be offered.

Altogether, three types were offered: a two-door hard-top, a two-door landau and a four-door landau. The four-door landau had a typically elegant landau roof, complete with sidebars that emulated the hardware of the canvas-top carriages of yore. This car echoed the Lincoln Continental in its use of doors that opened to the center, making the rear doors so-called 'suicide doors.' Loaded with standard features, 1967 Thunderbirds had a standard 315-hp, 390-ci (6.4 L) V-8, or an optional 345-hp, 428-ci (seven L) V-8.

Though the 1960s were not quite yet the days of 'virgin vinyl,' they were the days of 'vinyl, vinyl, everywhere.'

Chrysler's premier line, the Imperial, also offered its fair share of vinyl. In general, the Imperials of 1967–68 continued the pleasingly sharp-cornered styling of the previous few years, and added a subtle V-shaped grille in 1968.

As of 1968, the Chevrolet Caprice was firmly entrenched at the top of the Chevrolet full-size offerings. It had the

Above: A promotional photo of a 1967 Camaro SS 350 convertible. Note its 'Coke bottle' design, in imitation of the mid-1960s Pontiacs (see page 77).

Using non-words or 'designer' words to name cars was less widespread in the 1960s than it is today. Questions arose around the then-new designer word 'Camaro.' It was *very like*, but *was not*, a Spanish word for 'room.' General Motors finally said 'Camaro' was meant to 'connote friendliness'—and that it seemed like a good idea at the time.

Opposite: A 1968 Pontiac Firebird convertible.

A four-speed transmission, handling package and other goodies made both the Javelin and the AMX highly desirable items, and it didn't hurt matters when land speed record holder Craig Breedlove took a 1968 AMX to the Goodyear test track in Texas, and set 106 world speed records with the car.

The luxury market was proceeding apace, as well. Cadillac, ever the leader in American luxury car manufacture, executed a bold stroke in 1967, and the Eldorado gained a note of great distinction. The Oldsmobile Toronado front-wheel-drive chassis and running gear (except for the engine—a modified Cadillac power plant was used) was used as a base for a new edition of the Eldorado.

With this, the Eldorado became a front-wheel drive automobile, and was the first car ever to combine power variable-ratio power steering, Automatic Level Control and front-wheel drive. The front-wheel drive arrangement allowed the Eldorado to accommodate the same passenger load as other Cadillacs in a body of smaller dimensions.

same flowing lines as the 1966 model, and included the new Astro-ventilation system.

The lower-range Chevrolets, Biscayne and Bel Air, offered sedan and station wagon models, with a choice of six-cylinder or small-block V-8 engines.

The Ford LTD became its own line in 1967, and was offered in four-door hardtop and sedan—as well as two-door hardtop coupe—models. The standard engine for these cars was a 200-hp, 289-ci (4.7 L) V-8, coupled to a Select-shift Cruise-O-Matic transmission. An optional 315-hp, 390-ci (6.4 L) V-8 was available, as was power steering; power brakes; a tinted windshield; an AM/FM radio; air conditioning; and a host of other optional features. In 1968, the LTDs received a front-end styling change, giving them a more stately, squared-off, look.

The Custom line, with an array of sedans, held down the lower full-size Ford line, while a selection of station wagons—including Fairlane, Fairlane 500, Ranch Wagon, Custom Wagon and Country Squire variants—were offered to the family car market as well as the standard versions of other Ford models.

Mercury's lower-price full-size cars included the Monterey and the Montclair, offering sedans, coupes and—in the case of the former—a convertible. Station wagon models—the Commuter and the more-upscale Colony Park—were also offered. The Park Lane continued as Mercury's top-level offering until the introduction of the Marquis in 1967.

Pontiac's lower-price lines were represented by the Catalina and the Executive, which replaced the Star Chief in 1967. While the former also included a convertible style, both lines offered sedans, hardtops and station wagons.

The Pontiac Grand Prix was offered as a convertible as well as a two-door hardtop in 1967. This year, full-size Pontiac styling featured an arrow-like side shape, with a slanting crease emphasizing the rear quarter panels on either side, giving the cars a 'ready-to-launch' look. Hideaway headlights, semi-hidden front parking lamps and slot-like, horizontal tail lamps distinguished the Grand Prix styling that year, and standard features included luxuriant interior appointments, fender skirts, a notchback front bench seat with a center armrest and an imitation walnut burl dashboard.

In 1967, a fastback coupe was added to the Plymouth Sport Fury line, and in 1968, the VIP line gained additional

'Quieter than a Rolls-Royce.' *Above:* An advertisement for the 1968 Ford LTD, which had ceased being merely a high-level trim offering for the Galaxie 500 in 1967, and featured plush interior appointments, plus large, smooth-running engines such as Ford's 428-ci (seven-L) V-8.

Many Thunderbird enthusiasts were dismayed with the unwonted growth they saw in each new design change. Then, in 1967, came that moment that 'T-bird' fans had dreaded all along: Ford Motor Company produced a four-door Thunderbird.

Opposite: A 1967 Thunderbird four-door landau: not a bad-looking car, but an anathema to purists.

At right: A 1967 Chevrolet Impala SS convertible, evincing the popular body design that was introduced in 1965.

Below right: A 1964 Chevelle SS convertible. Compare this blunt design with the Impala just discussed.

Far right: A 1968 Ford Fairlane Torino GT, equipped with a 390-ci (6.4-L) V-8. The Torino's fastback roof was incongruous with its basically boxy styling, but Ford had an ulterior motive. The fastback added just a modicum of streamlining with which to get an advantage over General Motors and Chrysler Corporation rivals on the national stock car circuit. It was a cheap way to avoid having to spend a fortune on retooling for a more streamlined body style.

with three levels, and included sedans, coupes and station wagons. Also, the last convertibles of the 1960s to be offered by AMC were 1968 Rebels.

If anything, the compact/economy market was about to burst forth into new prominence, with the increased societal awareness that was then forming around the notions of 'clean air,' 'better mileage' and urban gridlock.

By 1967, the transition from the Rambler nomenclature to that of its parent company, American Motors Corporation ('AMC'), was complete. The American model was still the leading economy car of the company.

As for the Chevrolet Corvair, General Motors' directors had confronted Ralph Nader in court, and the subsequent publicity only emphasized the points he had made in his book. *Unsafe at Any Speed* caused such a furor that

models in the form of six- and nine-passenger station wagons, only to be cut back to four-door hardtop and two-door hardtop and fastback models by 1969, and then to be supplanted by an extended range of Fury offerings in 1970.

The lower-price full-size Belvedere and lower-level Furies were the cars to look toward for full-size family needs in the Plymouth line.

American Motors offered the full-size Ambassador in sedan, hardtop and station wagon variants, in three levels, the top two of which were the DPL and the SST. The SST was a V-8-only offering. These cars were literally loaded with standard equipment that would have been optional on many other makes.

Bringing up the intermediate-size part of the AMC market, the Rambler Rebel was represented by a full line, also

General Motors decided to let the Corvair program wind down.

For instance, 209,000 Corvairs were produced in 1965, but only 12,887 were produced in 1968. Previous to the *Unsafe At Any Speed* publicity, 1.5 million Corvairs were sold, but afterward, only 125,000 were. Chevrolet announced the cancellation of the Corvair program in May of 1969.

The Ford Falcon continued unabated, however. It was a popular family car, as well as seeing duty at the drag strip in a number of outrageous guises—including 427- (6.9 L) and 428-ci (seven L) Falcons.

Much the same could be said for the dramatically-styled Mercury Comets, similarly awash in an array of options, and capable of duties ranging from fuel-saving family car to fire-breathing tire destroyer. An upper-level version of the Comet, the Mercury Montego, was introduced in 1968.

The Plymouth Barracuda had stopped looking like a fastback Valiant, and that left the Valiant itself to tend to the business it was best suited for: general domestic duty. Plymouth's tried-and-true 230-hp, 318-ci (5.2 L) V-8 became a Valiant option for the first time in 1968.

The Chevy Nova grew to 190 inches in overall length in 1968. The body received a rather beautiful, flowing design with an extremely well-balanced profile. Though a 90-hp, 153-ci four-cylinder was offered, a 140-hp, 230-ci (3.7 L) six was the base power plant of choice, with performance options on the Nova Super Sport that essentially 'went through the roof,' some of which I have discussed previously.

The mid-to-late 1960s were the era of the fastback roof. Suddenly, every automaker had a fastback model or two (or three or four) in their lineup.

Above: An advertisement for the 1967 Marlin, advertising a range of 'Typhoon' V-8s. American Motors was more successful with their Javelin and AMX performance cars of 1968.

A LAST GASP, AND A QUICK TURN

Pollution was a mounting public concern as the 1960s drew to a close. Automakers could see the end of 'horsepower at any cost' in sight. It didn't look pretty to them, as they had millions invested in market plans and equipment that would be obsolete within a few years. Even so, the day of the massive engine was not over, but the day of detuning would soon begin.

Detuning was a process by which US automakers hoped to hedge their bets. Whereby the environmentalists were ready to do away with muscle cars and their ilk, automakers had an investment, after all, and there were still buyers for cars that had high cubic inches.

The trick was to give the buyer the ci, and to reduce the horsepower—and therefore, hopefully, the emissions—pleasing everybody. However, a huge engine is still a huge engine, and if it is made to run inefficiently, it will still produce monstrous amounts of pollution.

Conversely, if the huge engine does not deliver what the buyer requires of it, that buyer will not buy another such 'fake muscle car.' Therefore, this gambit on the part of automakers failed.

Another concern that contributed to the death of the 1960s-style muscle car was highway safety. Manufacturers caught on to the idea of 'good handling' too late. Much earlier than they finally did, automakers should have made their high-horsepower engines integral with a package that improved the cars' handling.

There was a definite problem in that many of the car-buyers who wanted to go fast didn't have the driving skill to handle their cars.

Among notable exceptions to the inadequate handling equipment problem were the Shelby Mustangs, which were built essentially for competition. However, much like General Motors' woes over the inadequately-designed early Corvairs, the advent of a remedy to the situation came too late on the part of US automakers.

Plus, to truly complete the prevention, each potential muscle car buyer would have had to be given a competition driving test and a psychological profile. Clearly, it was unlikely that such steps would have been instituted.

Therefore, even though the later muscle cars were more thoroughbreds than many of their 1960s predecessors, the end of the muscle car was also ordained by public safety concerns.

The end-of-the-1960s Pontiac look was that of a split grille and a nosepiece.

At right: A 1968 Pontiac LeMans GTO front end. The grille shell was made of hard rubber, and did double duty as a bumper. The base GTO engine this year was a 350-hp, 400-ci (6.5-L) V-8.

Opposite: A 1969 Firebird coupe. The chrome grille shell of this car rode on a hard-rubber base. Performance options ranged from the Sprint package—including a 230-hp, 250-ci (four-L) six-cylinder engine—to the Ram Air IV package—with a 345-hp, 400-ci (6.5-L) V-8. This was the same V-8 used in the Firebird Trans-Am package, which included competition handling equipment.

The turn of the decade out of the 1960s was curiously like the turn of the decade into the 1960s, in that an increased interest in economy encouraged automakers to produce new lower-level lines. As opposed to calling these little cars 'compacts,' as they had a decade earlier, automakers now called them 'economy cars.'

As for luxury cars—those who could afford them still wanted them, and so they were built, often as large as ever. For instance, *none* of the 1975 Cadillacs were under 5000 pounds.

Even though the overall 'picture' was rapidly changing, the muscle cars had not yet faded from the scene. There was to be a last hurrah for the 'street rockets' and 'highway missiles'—as some called the muscle cars.

Cosmetic change was all the rage among automakers. For instance, the 1969 Pontiac GTO acquired the plastic 'beak' nosepiece that was also installed that year on the company's Firebirds.

The year 1969 also saw the introduction of the Dodge Swinger with its high-performance 340-ci (5.6 L) engine, which was very popular among economy-minded performance fans.

The most ostentatious cars of 1969 were, however, the Dodge Daytona Charger and its counterpart, the Plymouth

Road Runner Super Bird, born of a need for better aerodynamics on the stock car track. Even the powerful Chrysler hemi couldn't catch the Fords, and it was decided that very, very slick aerodynamics were needed.

Hence, the Charger and the Super Bird each had an elongated, drooping nose and a high 'wing' spoiler on the rear deck. They were limited edition cars (1000 of each were sold to the general public). Much-intensified competition versions of these cars reached speeds of nearly 200 mph on the stock car tracks, while their more domestic brethren prowled the streets and highways, startling the public at large.

The year 1969 also saw the introduction of the 'Six-Pack' option for the 440 (7.2 L) wedge engine: three two-barrel carburetors that opened up in a manner similar to the setup on the original Pontiac GTOs.

The Chrysler hemi engine was discontinued after 1971, as Chrysler Corporation chose not to detune the engine to meet the stringent public transportation regulations that were coming into effect. However, even now it remains so popular that various machinists produce Chrysler hemi 'clones' for racing only.

As of 1969, Oldsmobile improved its 4-4-2s in offering its W-30 performance package for Cutlass and Cutlass

For the year 1969, Pontiac brought out an improvement for their already outstanding Tempest LeMans GTO. Since it already had a forced-air induction feature called 'Ram Air,' Pontiac engineers added to the GTO lineup with a higher-level model that had more performance goodies and a choice of two Ram Air V-8s—both 400-ci (6.5-L) units. This model was called 'The Judge,' after popular jargon of the period.

Opposite: A 1969 GTO coupe with the Ram Air IV feature.

At left: 'The Judge.' In 1969, it came in two models—a convertible, as shown here, and a coupe.

Supreme models. This package centered on a 350-ci (5.7 L) engine with forced air induction, which was claimed to produce 360 hp, and was one of the fastest factory-to-the-public cars of that year.

The Chevrolet Camaro with the Z28 package continued to be the delight of many a performance buff, and acquitted itself honorably on the Trans-Am circuit.

In 1969, the 400 (6.5 L) HO Pontiac Firebird became the 400 (6.5 L) Ram Air HO 11, which put out 340 hp (more for those carbuyers who removed the metal 'detuning tab' on the carburetor). This was also the year that the first Firebird Trans Am—so designated to take advantage of Pontiac's efforts in the Trans-Am racing series—was offered to the public.

The Firebird Trans Am became known for its spectacular decals, which included a spread-eagle 'firebird' on the hood. As outfitted for competition on the Trans-Am circuit, the Firebird had a 303-ci (4.9 L) V-8 with tunnel port heads, à la the NASCAR Fords.

AMC's performance offerings for 1969 included the Jav-

elin and the AMX, and a one-year-only special, the American SC/Rambler with a 315-hp high-compression 390-ci (6.4 L) V-8, four-speed transmission and a host of other performance items as standard equipment.

The Javelin continued to compete with success on the Trans-Am circuit, and full-race versions were released for the street market, as per the SCCA's homologation rules. The AMX, however, was soon to be dropped, as it had done all that AMC had wanted it to do: it had boosted the company's image in the eyes of the public, and would

continue on only as an honorific designation on certain models of the Javelin and the Hornet.

As I have said, however, American automakers were being pressured to make a change. Soon enough, public concerns for safety led to an overall curbing of performance horsepower on new models. While the Camaro, Mustang and Firebird—when purchased with the proper handling options, were fairly good-handling cars, many of their fellows were not—highway missiles that they were, they were seen as dangerous in the hands of unrestrained enthusiasm.

The early 1970s would see a host of the formerly mighty muscle cars merely parading as such, with detuned engines and hood scoops and decals galore.

However, the luxury cars would not so readily give up their extravagant dimensions, even in light of the looming gasoline crisis and growing concerns about pollution.

Cadillacs for the year 1969 bore the styling that had been created for the Eldorado the year before: subtly sloping rear window, blunt front and rear silhouettes, and headlights and grille inboard of the leading fender edges.

Opposite: A Z28 Camaro coupe. The first Z28s were only slightly tamer versions of the cars that competed on the Trans-Am auto-racing circuit. Their 302-ci (4.9-L) V-8s cranked out 350 hp, and were equipped with tuned exhaust pipes, competition handling equipment and high-efficiency drive train components.

Above: A 1969 Pontiac Firebird Trans-Am coupe. Unlike the Z28 Camaro, the Firebird Trans-Am was equipped with a 400-ci (6.5-L) V-8, while the Firebirds that *really* raced on the Trans-Am circuit had 303-ci (4.9-L) V-8s.

The 1969 Calais 682 model line was composed of a two-door coupe and a four-door sedan—both with six-passenger capacity. They featured the then-standard 472-ci (7.7 L) Cadillac V-8, with 375 hp. Also standard on these cars were headrests; variable-ratio power steering and dual power brakes.

The 1969 Cadillac Eldorado, officially known as Fleetwood Eldorado, was a six-passenger, two-door hardtop on a 129.5-inch wheelbase, the same as the Calais and DeVille.

The Eldorado's standard equipment was that of the Fleetwood line, plus power-operated rear vent windows. Optional equipment for 1969 Cadillacs included air conditioning (standard on some); vinyl roofs in various colors; seat warmers; power seats; bucket seats; door bumper guards; floor mats; Automatic Level Control; Cruise Control; leather upholstery; an AM/FM stereo radio; a Guide-Matic headlamp control and a host of other options—all aimed at making the passenger feel secure in knowing that his or her automotive environment would be everything they could hope for in the realm of style and luxury.

By 1969, the Chrysler Imperial line had lost much of its Lincoln-inspired slab-sidedness, and featured a long, low, look, with blunt ends. This was known as 'fuselage' styling, and was characterized by a slipperiness of detail that included wraparound taillights molded into the rear bumper, which was molded into the rear deck. The headlights were hideaway units hidden behind a gridwork grille. The rear window sloped dramatically, in a semi-fastback styling.

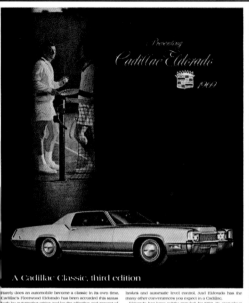

A Cadillac Classic, third edition

Rarely does an automobile become a classic in its own time. Cadillac's Fleetwood Eldorado has been accorded this status both by automotive critics and by the affection and respect of the motoring public.

Only Eldorado combines the precision of front-wheel drive with the performance of the largest production V-8 engine in any passenger car. In fact, morning's newest advances are standard, including variable-ratio power steering, front disc brakes and automatic level control. And Eldorado has the many other conveniences you expect in a Cadillac.

Eldorado has been subtly restyled for 1969. Its marvelous new interiors, including a dramatic new 'control center' instrument panel, make driving an even more delightful experience. Your dealer will be glad to demonstrate its thrilling performance and incomparable ride. You'll see why Eldorado has fully earned its designation, 'World's Finest Personal Car.'

Above: An advertisement for the 1969 Cadillac Fleetwood Eldorado, proclaiming the 'largest production V-8 engine in any passenger car'—a 500-ci (8.2-L) V-8 that produced 400 hp. The Eldorado had become a front-wheel-drive car in 1967, and *that* feature was also a major selling point.

At right: A 1969 Cadillac Convertible DeVille. Metallic gold was then, and is still, a popular big-car color.

Imperial offerings for 1969 were streamlined down to the Crown and the LeBaron series. The engine for both lines was the 350-hp, 440-ci (7.2 L) V-8, mated to the dependable Chrysler Torqueflite transmission.

The Crown Imperial series had standard equipment including power front disk brakes; power steering; power windows; an electric clock; carpeting; and a remote-control sideview mirror. The types offered were six passenger cars of the four-door sedan and two- and four-door hardtop varieties.

The LeBaron differed from the Crown in that it featured a vinyl roof and a formal rear window. LeBaron variants were two- and four-door hardtops. Cloth and leather bench seats and storage compartments in all doors were standard on the LeBaron.

Above: The American Motors Javelin. This car did what the unsuccessful Marlin could not—it sold well, and was truly a versatile car, available as a six-cylinder 'grocery getter' or a V-8 high-performance coupe.

In competition form, it often led the field in Trans-Am racing, and nearly wrested the championship from the reigning Mustang Trans-Am team.

At left: The 1969 American Motors AMX, which was a smaller version of the American Motors Javelin, and was the first two-passenger, steel-bodied American car since the 1955—57 Ford Thunderbirds. Craig Breedlove established 106 world speed records with an AMX. The base-level engine was a 290-ci (4.7-L) V-8. The most powerful AMX engine available was a 315-hp, 390-ci (6.4-L) V-8.

The first big styling change for the Lincoln Continental of the late 1960s came in 1969, with the advent of the Mark III, which hearkened back to the Continental Mark II of 1956–57, with its personable 'coupe' styling, and sporty spare tire hump on the rear deck lid. A beak-like radiator grille completed the impression of a well-proportioned car that was eminently stylish.

In fact, the Mark III's styling belied its size. This emphasized one of the several points of departure for the Ford and General Motors styling departments. General Motors, when dealing with a large car, made every effort to enhance the feeling of size and bulk—trying to make a virtue of excess. On the other hand, when Ford's stylists were at their best, the effect was a visual reduction of bulk, a sleight of hand that is as classically modern as the General Motors approach is classically baroque.

The year 1969 also saw the last of the 1961 Continental-style cars, as both the Continental—in two-door coupe and four-door sedan—and the Continental Mark III—in two-door coupe configuration—were offered.

The 1969 Continental Mark III featured many of the standard items offered on the Continental, plus individually adjustable front seats; front and rear center folding armrests; a flow-through ventilation system; and a rear lamp monitoring system. By way of comparison, the 1969 Continental was set upon a wheelbase of 126 inches, and was 224 inches overall; while the Continental Mark III had a wheelbase of 117.2 inches, and was 216 inches overall.

In the realm of only slightly less luxurious full-size cars, the market was going strong. The time would come that these 'baby behemoths' would be snubbed in favor of smaller cars by the upwardly-mobile sectors of the public, while families would choose simpler, and less expensive, versions of them.

The 1969 AMC Ambassador was still the top-of-the-line car for that company, while the mid-size Rebel offered sedans, coupes and station wagons for two trim levels,

At left: **A 1969 Continental Mark III two-door coupe. Introduced in April of 1968, the Mark III was nonetheless billed as a 1969 model. Reminiscent of the fabulous 1956—57 Continental Mark II, the Mark III had a spare tire hump—and short-deck, long-hood styling.**

Rebel and Rebel SST. The Ambassador was available in three trim levels, Ambassador proper, Ambassador DPL and Ambassador SST.

Buick was doing reasonably well in the market with its full-size offerings. The 1969 Electra 225 featured a body that had a graceful trimline that ran from the bottom rear quarter panel to the upper front quarter panel on both sides. Bright metal accent was used on the rocker panels from rear to front, and fender skirts contributed to the rakish effect at the rear. This style worked best with two-door hardtops, but seemed a bit massive for four-door types.

The Electra 225 Custom was Buick's top of the line in 1969. Four types were offered: four-door sedan and hardtop, two-door hardtop and convertible. The standard engine and transmission was a 360-hp, 430-ci (seven L) V-8 attached to a Turbo-Hydramatic 400 transmission.

For 1969, Chevrolet Caprices received a squared-off look, and this was changed back to a more open look—with a slanting front bumper accenting a pointed nose, for

1970. That year, the factory price for a four-door hardtop was $3527.

Chrysler New Yorker offerings for the year 1969 included a two-door hardtop coupe, a four-door hardtop sedan and a four-door sedan. The station wagon offerings of earlier years were now consolidated under a separate series, known as Town & Country. These were, for two previous years, included with the bottom-range Newport offerings. However, Chrysler apparently had revived the notion of the truly upscale station wagon: the Town & Country wagons for that year were very posh.

Chrysler bodies featured 'fuselage styling,' which is also discussed previously in this text. Each carbody was a tapering, fuselage-style unit, with convex sheet metal sides (as opposed to the semi-concave side sheet metal of the mid-1960s). The body's 'heavier rear, lighter front' effect recalled the early 1960s Dodge and Plymouth lines. This touch gave the large New Yorker a somewhat racy look, and avoided the over-heaviness that such as the Buicks traditionally have had.

The stock 1969 New Yorker engine was a 350-hp, 440-ci (7.2 L) V-8, mated to a Torqueflite transmission. The same was true of the Town & Country wagons, and the 300 Series itself.

Also near decade's end, the 1969 Dodge Monaco shared the Chrysler's new fuselage styling. The Monaco had, as standard features: full seat belts and front shoulder harnesses; a full interior lighting complement; all vinyl interior trim for two- and four-door hardtops; cloth and vinyl interior trim for sedans and station wagons; and a power tailgate window for station wagons.

Dodge's lower-price full-size line, the Coronet, was available in two trim levels, and in a wide variety of sedans, coupes and station wagons, including some of the muscle cars I have mentioned earlier.

Ford continued to offer its LTD. The basic 1969 Ford LTD power plant was a 220-hp, 302-ci (4.9 L) V-8 coupled to a Select-Shift Cruise-O-Matic transmission. This year, five models were offered: two four-door sedans, one two-door fastback coupe, one six-passenger station wagon and one 10-passenger station wagon.

The Mercury Marquis moved into full series status in 1969, offering four-door sedan, hardtop and station wagon models, as well as two-door hardtop and convertible models.

Generally, a front-end treatment that featured Lincoln Continental-like subtleties and hideaway headlights; dual lower-body pinstripes; a solid row of rectangular taillights; deep-pile upholstery; burled-walnut-like interior paneling and accents; and a full courtesy light complement distinguished the Marquis series.

Lower-price full- and mid-size Mercurys such as the Monterey, Custom and Montego lines offered sedans, coupes and station wagons, with a full array of optional equipment to suit any carbuyer's specifications.

For Oldsmobile, Cutlass, Delta Eighty-Eight and Vista Cruiser wagons held down the lower-price full- and intermediate-range share of the market. The Ninety-Eight was still the highest level in the late 1960s.

The Ninety-Eight for 1969 was offered in six types. Four-door types included two kinds of sedans and two-door types included a coupe and a convertible.

As for Pontiac's entry into the lower-level luxury field, the convertible was dropped from the Grand Prix offerings, and 1969 saw an all-new Grand Prix on an exclusive, 119-inch wheelbase. This new Grand Prix also had such distinguishing features as a V-shaped grille, square headlamp trim and an ultra-long hood.

The aircraft-inspired interior included full dashboard and courtesy lighting; bucket seats; carpeted lower door panels; a padded dash/console unit; hidden windshield wipers with 'pulse' action; and a floor-mounted shift lever.

Though these cars were available with either a three- or four-speed Synchromesh transmission, the overwhelming preference among buyers was an automatic transmission, pointing to the fact that these were far more luxury cars than muscle cars, despite their sporty looks.

The Catalina, Bonneville and Executive lines, (this last had replaced the Star Chief line), offered sedans, hardtops and station wagons for the lower-price Pontiac full-size market, while the Catalina and Bonneville also offered convertibles.

Full-size Plymouths, such as the Furies and the VIP, received a heavier-looking, squared-off body treatment for the late 1960s, and also were given horizontal quad headlights in 1969.

Intermediates like the Belvedere, Road Runner, Satellite, Sport Satellite and GTX had sleeker styling, with hints of a 'Coke bottle' shape in the side profile, and had horizontal quad headlights for years.

The 1969 Buick Riviera sported bright-metal wheel well and rocker panel trim. Bench seats had been offered as optional for front seating for some years. Expanded vinyl was a standard interior appointment, and custom interiors included a choice of bench, notchback or bucket front seats with the highest-quality vinyl and/or vinyl-and-cloth combination.

The base factory price for the 1969 Riviera was $5331—up approximately $100 from the previous year, and up $1000 from the Riviera's first model year, 1963.

Oldsmobile's Toronado for 1969 had a 375-hp, 455-ci (7.4 L) engine mated to a Turbo-Hydramatic transmission. Other standard features included power brakes; power steering; an electric clock; full carpeting; and flow-through ventilation. The styling for 1969 hardened the Toronado's lines a bit, making sharp delineations where once were softly flowing curves—in this, it brought the Toronado in line with many of General Motors' other offerings for that year.

Then again, there were the real winners of the 'end of the 1960s' sweepstakes—the compact economy cars. How-

ever, many of these little autos were eliminated in favor of new concepts as to what a small, low-priced and economical car might be.

Ford Falcons remained essentially the same as they had since the mid-1960s, and were dropped from the Ford line in 1970, but the name was then used for a budget version of the Torino—before being dropped altogether.

A new note was struck before the Falcon's demise, however—this was the all-new 1969 Maverick, which was a fastback, long-nosed car of 179.4 inches (4.5 meters) overall length that rode on a Falcon chassis. The Maverick was meant to be direct competition for the Volkswagen. It was available in only one style—a two-door sedan—and was powered by a 170-ci (2.7 L) six-cylinder power plant.

The Chevy II name was dropped from the Chevrolet lineup in 1969, and its lineage—now considered a 'senior compact'—was carried on by the Nova series. The year 1971 saw the advent of the Chevrolet Vega, which was an all-new line of sub-compact cars, and was offered in sedan, coupe and station wagon models.

Ford's Mustang continued on as a two-door in hardtop, convertible and fastback models. As I have said, you could order your Mustang any way you wanted it, but it soon lost its appeal as Ford's designers made the Mustang bigger and bulkier.

Even at that, the compact cars I have discussed here would be altered or outright supplanted, in time, by increasingly economical models that ironically were as dangerous in their own way—cheap construction, failure of quality control and dangerously underpowered design—as the 'highway missiles' of the muscle car period.

As for them, the performance-oriented muscle cars surely had to kneel to the changing marketplace. Emblematic of this were the 302-ci (4.2 L) and 350-ci (5.7 L) V-8s that were offered for Mustangs of 1973: the 302 had 136 hp—what most six-cylinder engines were putting out a decade before—and the 350 put out a 'slack-muscle' 156 hp. The Mustang itself became the Pinto-like Mustang II in 1974.

A wild-blue-yonder kind of excitement: Olds Cutlass S

Above: An advertisement underscoring the ersatz aeronautical thrill of driving a 1969 Oldsmobile Cutlass S coupe. The first Oldsmobile V-8, an overhead-valve power plant of 303 ci (4.9 L), was introduced in 1949. Dubbed the 'Rocket V-8,' it was the progenitor of such as the 350-ci (5.7-L) 'Rocket V-8' advertised here.

At left: A 1969 Chevrolet Nova coupe, available with engines ranging from a 90-hp, 153-ci (2.5-L) four-cylinder unit to Chevrolet's popular 200-hp, 307-ci (five-L) V-8. For high-performance fans, there was a 300-hp, 350-ci (5.7-L) V-8 that was part of the Nova SS option package.

THE BEST OF THE INTERNATIONAL SCENE

The love affair with fast cars extended far beyond the boundaries of the United States. Across the Atlantic in Great Britain, Jaguar introduced the XKE in 1961. Available as a roadster or a two-seat coupe, the sleek XKE featured a 3.8-L (231.9 ci) power plant and reached a top speed of 150 mph (241 kph), going from zero to 100 mph in less than 16 seconds. In 1964, the XKE was fitted with a 4.2-L (256.3 ci) engine.

Britain's answer to the United States' popular Ford Mustang was the MGB GT. A success from the start, the GT offered good looks and high performance at an excellent price—£998 in Britain and $3000 in the United States.

A more expensive sports car was the Aston Martin DB5. Introduced in 1963, the DB5 featured a four-L (244 ci), 280 hp engine and was offered as a convertible with an optional automatic transmission.

In addition to building some of the world's finest sports cars, Britain was positioned at the forefront of both the economy car trend and the luxury car market. On the economy end of the scale was the BMC Mini. While there was nothing new about the Mini's features—rack-and-pinion steering, front-wheel drive, transverse engine—what made it exceptional was that the entire package was so much better than other manufacturers' attempts.

At the opposite end of the spectrum were the luxury cars of Rolls-Royce. The new decade marked the arrival of the Silver Cloud II, equipped with a V-8 engine and standard automatic transmission and power steering. The Silver Cloud III, which made its debut in 1962, was eight percent more powerful due to a higher compression rate. In appearance, the III differed from the II only slightly, featuring four headlights and a lower hood line.

Meanwhile, Italy, as represented by Ferrari, was attracting the attention of sports car and racing enthusiasts with their fast, sexy cars. The 275 GTB and the 275 GTS were unveiled at the Paris Salon in October 1964. They were the first Ferraris to feature independent suspension. But the most exciting Ferrari of the decade was the 365 GTB/4, better known as the Daytona. Introduced in 1968, the Daytona was one of the fastest road cars ever made.

In Germany, Porsche continued its tradition of greatness with the introduction of the brutish 911 in 1964. The successor to the 356, the 911 featured several innovations, most notably a six-cylinder, air-cooled engine.

Opposite: **Powered by the race-proven XK engine, the Jaguar XKE was introduced in 1961. The six-cylinder XK engine was a versatile power plant—smooth and powerful; it was ideal for use in sport cars, sedans and racing cars alike.**

The E-type Jaguar had one of the sleekest body designs yet seen anywhere in the world. Rivaled only by the Italian Ferraris in styling and performance, the XKE could be purchased for merely a third of the cost of the least expensive Ferrari!

These pages: Examples of Britain's finest contributions to the world of motoring in the 1960s.

Far left: The 1969 version of the Morgan 4/4. Based on the design first introduced in 1935, the Morgan 4/4 has been produced in slightly modified versions for more than 50 years. The 1969 model was powered by a 1.6-L (97.6-ci) Ford UK engine and capable of speeds around 100 mph (161 kph).

Left: The front-wheel drive BMC Mini-Cooper won many a road rally, a testament to its astonishing road holding, handling and stability. The most thoughtfully designed small car of its time, the BMC Mini had a surprisingly spacious interior and yet had an overall length of only 10 feet! Its radical engineering sparked a revolution in the design of compact cars.

Right: Introduced at the 1962 London Motor Show, the MGB followed in the footsteps of the highly acclaimed MGA sports car of the 1950s. The MGB was a definite improvement over the MGA in terms of driver comfort. It had a roomier interior and featured winding windows—a first for an open cockpit MG. It had the excellent handling of the MGA with improved performance, bettering the MGA's top speed by five mph (eight kph) and with considerably better acceleration.

The MGB GT II shown *at right* belongs to arch MG enthusiast John Thornley.

Left: A 1962 Rolls-Royce Silver Cloud II saloon. The Silver Cloud II marked the introduction of the V-8 engine as a power plant in Rolls-Royce automobiles. Automatic transmission and power steering were both standard equipment on the Silver Cloud II. It shared the body style of its predecessor, the Silver Cloud, first introduced in 1955 as a replacement for the Silver Dawn model. The Silver Cloud series itself was replaced by the Silver Shadow in 1965.

Bearing the initials of the man who resurrected the Aston Martin company after the end of World War II, David Brown's DB series of sports cars began with the DB2 of 1950. After a decade of racing experience and on-going refinement the DB5 (*at right*) was unveiled.

The DB5 came equipped with a four-L (244-ci) engine (*below*) that produced in excess of 280 hp and was available with an automatic transmission.

The DB5 was made famous by its appearances in the films *Goldfinger* and *Thunderball*. James Bond's Aston Martin is best remembered for its unique special equipment: rotating license plates, hydraulic rams, machine guns built into the front fenders, bulletproof screen in the rear deck, a facility to dispense an oil slick, smokescreen or nails, and last but not least the ejector seat for disposing of unwanted passengers.

Left: Germany's leading sports car manufacturer, Porsche, debuted its 911 model in 1964 as the successor to its legendary Porsche 356 series. The rear-mounted air-cooled 2.2-L (134-ci) six-cylinder engine of the 911C shown here was equipped with Bosch mechanical fuel injection.

Below: The NSU Ro80 of 1967 was the first production car powered by a Wankel twin-rotor rotary engine.

Right: The Mercedes-Benz 280SE 4.5 saloon. The 280SE was one of 'The New Generation' of Mercedes-Benz cars presented to the public in 1968. The company described the cars' engines as '...not primarily designed to attain maximum top speeds but to produce a higher torque to help keep traffic moving and to provide quiet running and flexibility as a means of relieving the driver (of stress and fatigue).'

The Ferrari company of Modena, Italy is known around the world for its stylish award-winning racing cars. They have also produced some of the finest road-going sport cars.

Left: Unveiled at the Paris Salon in October of 1964, the 275GTB was one of the first Ferraris to have four-wheel independent suspension.

Below: Considered by some to be the 'most civilized' of Ferrari's gran turismo models, the 330 GTC was introduced in 1965. It was powered by a four-L (244-ci) V12 engine.

Opposite: Debuted in 1968, the Ferrari 365 GTB/4 is one of the fastest road cars in the world with a proven top speed of 174 mph (280 kph)!

The cars produced in Australia during the 1960s were utilitarian in design. Saloons (sedans) and wagons best satisfied the needs of the broadest section of the Australian car-buying public.

Below: The Ford XR Falcon Fairmont sedan. Ford offered optional V-8 power in 1966, two years ahead of Holden. The XR Falcon, with its long wheelbase, was wildly popular. Customers flocked to the showrooms, and dealers placed many advance orders for the new Ford.

Right: Soon after its introduction in 1963, the EH Holden began to sell in huge numbers, eventually becoming the best-ever selling Holden, with 256,969 sold in 18 months, and a monthly sales rate in excess of 14,000 units!

Opposite: Holden's offerings for 1968: the HB Torana (left), the HK wagon (center), and the HK saloon. Five-L (305-ci) and 5.3-L (323-ci) Chevrolet-built V-8 engines were offered as options on the HK models, a first for Holden cars.

INDEX